THE SERVICE PATH

Your Roadmap For Building Strong Customer Loyalty!

TERESA ALLEN • TRACY BROWN • REGINA CLARK
TIGER HARRISON • CARL HERRICK • JANA HIGH
MICHAEL HOFFMAN • JP MARONEY • BARBARA SANFILIPPO
BERNADETTE VADURRO • KELLI VRLA • RHONDA WILDMAN

MaroCom

MaroCom Publishing Company
A division of JPMaroney International

For information contact:
MaroCom Publishing Company
c/o JP Maroney International
PO Box 9492
Tyler, Texas 75711-9492
1-800-304-5758
www.JPMaroney.com

Learn about other titles in The Path Series℠ at www.PathSeries.com

FIRST EDITION

MaroCom™ Books in *The Path Series*℠

The Service Path:
Your Roadmap For Building Strong Customer Loyalty!

The Leadership Path:
Your Roadmap For Leading People In The 21st Century!

The Productivity Path:
Your Roadmap For Improving Employee Performance!

The Communication Path:
Your Roadmap For Building Rapport And Getting Ideas Across!

The Wellness Path:
Your Roadmap For Healthy, Happy Living!

The Teambuilding Path:
Your Roadmap for Creating Highly Productive Teams!

Check for additional titles online at http://www.PathSeries.com

TABLE OF CONTENTS

TABLE OF CONTENTS

INTRODUCTION

When I pulled together the eleven co-authors who joined me in writing this book, I commissioned them with one objective; answer the question...

"What can organizations do to build strong customer loyalty?"

The result is a book which contains twelve distinct, yet complimentary perspectives on the topic of providing effective customer service.

You will find a number of ideas, techniques, principles and strategies within the pages of this book. I suggest you select one or two ideas you believe will work for you, and then try them. Put them into action, and see if they do in fact increase your effectiveness in retaining customers.

If you want to go further, we've included contact information for each co-author on the first page of their chapter. Each co-author is a recognized expert in their field, and most provide additional services like: professional speaking, training, and consulting.

At the back of the book, you'll also find listings of other resources available from co-authors including: books, audio and video programs, assessment tools, and professional development systems.

I hope you find this book enlightening, inspiring, and highly useful in your quest to build strong customer loyalty.

Best of Success,
JP Maroney
Co-Author & Publisher

PS: Look for other titles in *The Path Series*℠ at www.PathSeries.com

CHAPTER ONE

Customer Conflict: Opportunity Knocks!

How to Turn Customer Dissatisfaction Into Customer Retention

Teresa Allen

A master storyteller and award-winning presenter, Teresa Allen weaves life experiences with business principles into captivating presentations that touch the mind and heart while inspiring improved performance.

"Success for any business is built one transaction at a time," says Allen. "The key is to have a passion for customers and the ability to understand what makes them tick. Those who master the art of communicating effectively will always be a step ahead of the competition!"

Owner of Success Strategies, a national training and consulting firm, Teresa is a member of the National Speakers Association and has been awarded the Professional Trainer of the Year Award from the American Society for Training and Development.

Popular Keynote Presentations:

- Common Sense Service
- Close Encounters on the Front Lines
- Keys to Successful Communication
- The Leadership Success M.A.P.
- Adding L.I.F.E. to Your Meetings

Success Strategies
Shreveport, LA • 800-797-1580 • www.AllenSpeaks.com

Teresa Allen

Customer Conflict: Opportunity Knocks!

How to Turn Customer Dissatisfaction Into Customer Retention

Most of us dread customer conflicts and complaints. No matter how many customers we satisfy during the day, the one we will think about all night is the customer who expressed dissatisfaction. The human mind easily concentrates on the negative.

Instead of surrounding yourself with such negative forces, try to consciously start each day with positive thoughts. Make a commitment today to change your early morning habits toward positive thoughts and it can literally change the course of your day, if not your life. It is up to each of us, to take control not only of our actions, but also of our thoughts and attitude.

To confront any difficult situation, a positive attitude is a must! Even armed with a positive attitude, you will need to prepare in advance for different types of complaints and conflicts. This chapter will provide resources that will enable you to turn conflicts into opportunities.

CALMING THE UPSET CUSTOMER

Have you ever felt that your customer was half-brained? Surprisingly enough, this could be true! When we are very upset, the left side of our brain, which controls logic, literally shuts down. This leaves only the right side, which controls our emotions. Thus, trying to reason with such an individual will be a wasted effort. We must use the following steps to calm the customer before proposing any solution based in logic or requiring reasoning.

1. Keep Yourself Calm / Focus on Facts

Upset customers can be downright vicious in an attempt to tell you what you have done wrong. The result is predictable. The service provider is offended and enters the combat mode.

How can this be avoided? To keep calm you must listen for content and not for the verbal assaults.

Example:

"You people are totally incompetent. I have called three times and you still can't get my account balance right..."

While you should be focusing on the three calls and incorrect balance, the natural tendency is to dwell on the "incompetent" remark. If you are not careful, you may miss the heart of the complaint.

2. Listen with Empathy

This step is often mishandled. Empathy is quite different from sympathy. Sympathy is "I'm sorry". 'Sorry' is a dangerous word if used too soon in a customer conflict situation.

In all the famous trials of the past decade, do you recall a single defendant uttering the words "I'm sorry?" Why not? 'Sorry' implies guilt. Too often, this is the first response to a complaint. If 'sorry' is used too soon, negotiation leverage can be severely damaged.

What then, should be the response? An empathetic response sounds more like this: "I certainly regret the inconvenience". This shows you understand how the customer feels without admitting guilt in advance of knowing all the facts.

3. Introduce Yourself and Ask for the Customer's Name

Many people forget this critical step. Conflict situations rarely begin with polite introductions. After listening to the complaint, you should give a statement of empathy, followed immediately by introducing yourself and asking the customer's name.

This process will tend to disarm the customer, especially if they are upset with your company. Now you have two people talking to each other instead of a company and a customer. As a result, the conversation will be more personal and will tend to remain civilized.

4. Restate the Customer Concern in Your Own Words

When someone issues a complaint, they have often practiced their recitation at least mentally, and sometimes verbally, prior to reaching you. Thus, they are able to spit it out at warp speed! It is your responsibility to make sure that nothing has been lost in the translation. To avoid any confusion, restate your understanding of the situation prior to making any response. If you do not, your solution may be off base and could prove to be unsatisfactory to the customer. Be sure to ask the customer to confirm your version prior to suggesting a solution.

5. Find a Win-Win Solution

Have you ever been tempted to gloat over winning an argument with a customer in a conflict situation? The most you can hope for is to win the short-term battle and lose the war to a competitor in the long run.

Quoting policies and telling a customer what you can't do will not help to build future business opportunities. For everything you can't do, there is something you can do. Find that and you may have a stronger relationship than the one you had prior to the conflict or complaint.

COMPLAINTS: INSTITUTIONAL VS. TRANSACTIONAL

The steps just reviewed are appropriate for transactional complaints. Transactional complaints center on a specific transaction with a single customer or are the result of the less than favorable actions of an employee. An institutional complaint relates to the way you do business as a whole rather than around events in a specific transaction. You must take a slightly different approach when a customer issues this type of complaint.

On a recent trip to Wal-Mart, I found myself in a checkout line behind eight other shoppers. Each had a cart filled to the rim. During my fifteen-minute wait, my eyes angrily scanned the twenty plus registers obviously designed to take money from customers. Only four were staffed with cashiers. Finally arriving at the front of the line, I vented my frustration to the cashier.

"Why don't you have more lines open?" I asked. "This is ridiculous!" What was her reply? "I'm going as fast as I can!"

Not quite the answer I wanted to hear! When a customer voices an institutional complaint, they are usually doing so with full realization that nothing can be done to solve the problem during their transaction.

In my situation, I knew the clerk did not make staffing decisions for Wal-Mart. What then, did I expect from her? First, I expected some empathy for the inconvenience I had just experienced. Second, I wanted her to validate my concern by telling me that she would pass it on to someone of higher authority.

Contrast this experience with the following encounter at a restaurant. Upon my arrival, I requested a non-smoking table. The response from the hostess was, "I'm sorry, but our non-smoking section is full. There will be about a thirty-minute wait. If you would prefer, I can seat you immediately in smoking."

What the hostess didn't know is that I had heard the very same response at this restaurant just a week earlier. Even though the hostess was polite and had given me the power of choice, (to wait or to be seated in a cloud of smoke), I was frustrated.

"You know, this has happened to me before," I replied. "Your non-smoking section obviously fills up faster than your smoking...shouldn't you make your non-smoking section larger?"

She replied with a genuine look of concern, "I have noticed that. I appreciate your suggestion and will pass it on to our manager. He is always interested in feedback from our customers. Would you like to speak with him personally?"

"No," I replied, my anger now diffused, "but I do appreciate your passing on my concern."

Only a small percentage of customers will take the time and effort to voice institutional complaints. The customers who do may very well be the tip of the iceberg of customer dissatisfaction.Your company and your front-line employees will be better off if there is a specific plan on how to handle institutional complaints.

If the steps suggested here are followed and management is informed, your job is not done. Management must track such complaints. If a large number of similar institutional complaints are registered, action should be taken to change the way business is conducted in that particular area.

CONTROLLED, EXPRESSED AND IRRATIONAL ANGER

Controlled Anger

On the surface, you might wish that all of your customers were calm and controlled when voicing complaints. In reality, this controlled anger can present the greatest challenge. Customers in a controlled state of anger are often holding back, not telling you exactly why they are upset.

Example:

Service Rep: "How are you doing today Mrs. Jones?"
Mrs. Jones: "Fine." (with a tone that screams NOT FINE!!)
Service Rep: "Is there anything I can help you with?"
Mrs. Jones: "Yes, but you'll probably mess it up!"

Ouch! If you are the service representative, you don't know whether Mrs. Jones is mad at her husband, her dog, or you! You can either hope she takes care of her business, and moves out of your day, or you can probe to find out what has caused her sour demeanor. Should it turn out to be a complaint against your business, you can then work on a solution. If you allow the cause of her anger to remain hidden, you may lose her business forever.

One word of caution before we leave the customer who is in a controlled state of anger. Many industries today have their own "lingo". Be very careful in any conflict situation not to use trade lingo that may confuse the customer. One sure way to vault a customer from controlled anger to expressed anger is to make them feel stupid by using words and terms unfamiliar to them! Take a moment to think of a few words or phrases that are used in your industry that may not be familiar to your customer. Make a mental note to leave these out of any explanations or justifications in a conflict scenario.

Expressed Anger

This individual has no problem telling you exactly what you did wrong and how you need to fix it. As a matter of fact, they may choose to entertain all your other customers with their recitation as well!

What should you do with this 'special' individual? (Notice I did not ask what you would LIKE to DO with him or her!) The first priority is to get the person off their stage. Be careful how you do this.

If you say, "Let's go to my office where we will have more privacy", the customer may get furious and launch into an even louder tirade. Instead, validate the concern with a response such as this: "Mr. Carlson, I certainly think your complaint deserves our immediate attention. You are one of our most important customers. Let's go to my office and see if we can find a solution."

Once in a more private setting, the customer's anger level should drop down to a controlled state. A solution can then be found through use of the calming techniques discussed earlier.

Irrational Anger

No matter what your line of business, you will eventually have to handle a customer in an irrational state of anger. In customer service seminars, I am often asked, "Do I have to listen to rude people using bad language?" My response is simple: NO! You do, however, need to have a game plan for just this type of situation. If you have used the calming steps and the customer is still ranting and raving, (and you are unable to escort them to a place of privacy), it is now up to you to confront them. This should first be done with a facial expression that tells the customer you heard what was said but are choosing not to respond to the inappropriate language.

If this does not work, tell the customer that you would like to help, but cannot if the bad language, which is offensive to both you and your other customers, continues. This should immediately be followed by the question, "Will you allow me to help you?" If the answer is no, you should quickly enlist the help of a co-worker or supervisor.

Be careful here...if your God-given instincts are setting off alarms telling you the irrational anger is caused by a source other than a bad day or a bad transaction, use whatever security measures you have established to immediately remove the person from your place of business. None of the techniques discussed in this chapter will help a person with mental illness or a drug or alcohol induced rage.

CONFLICT TRIGGERS: A WAR OF WORDS

Your choice of words can determine success or failure in a conflict situation. As a matter of fact, conflict can sometimes be generated by a particular combination of words. Think about it. Do you have trigger words that you hate to hear when you are the customer? My personal favorite is "Ma'am, our policy…" usually followed by "You have to…". A similar response from customers will result from words such as 'can't', 'won't', and 'problem'. These words all share a negative connotation. When trying to turn around a negative situation, concentrate on positive wording.

Example: (negative wording)

"Mr. Smith, I can't help you with this problem. Our policy states that your payment must reach us by the 15th in order to avoid late charges."

Most customers could care less about your policies. What do they care about? They want to know how you are going to address their concern.

Example: (positive wording)

"Mr. Smith, I can understand why you would want to avoid late charges. May I suggest that you mail your payment by the 10th so you can avoid our late charges which are processed on the 15th. We do appreciate your business, Mr. Smith!"

I was recently in a doctor's office that seemed to be more interested in educating patients on their policies than curing them of their ailments. There were so many signs posted around the reception window, it took about five minutes to read all of them:

SIGN IN AND HAVE A SEAT
COPAY REQUIRED BEFORE SEEING THE DOCTOR
NEW PATIENTS MUST HAVE PROOF OF INSURANCE
PATIENTS SEEN BY APPOINTMENT ONLY

Then there was the sign without words…an opaque window that blocked the waiting area from the reception desk. To me that sign said, "We're too busy to have to look at you!" or "Please don't interrupt my day!"

Our customers begin forming an impression of our level of service from the moment of first contact. What is the message you are sending? Is it building confidence in your business, or is it distributing ammunition for a conflict weapon of mass destruction?

Conflict Trigger Words to Avoid

- Policy
- You have to . . .
- Can't
- Won't

OPPORTUNITY KNOCKS...IS ANYONE HOME?

Are you part of a learning organization or a hiding organization when it comes to conflict? Does your organization encourage an open and frank discussion about mistakes when they happen, or are mistakes kept quiet due to fear of punishment?

In most companies, you will find at least one self-proclaimed expert who never makes a mistake. This person is seldom a very valuable employee. The reason they never make a mistake is because they rarely do anything! If you are a dedicated employee, committed to customer satisfaction through action, you will make mistakes. As long as you learn from your mistakes, they will build opportunities for enhanced customer relationships.

Many organizations now have SWOT team meetings on a regular basis. SWOT stands for Strengths, Weaknesses, Opportunities and Threats. Mistakes are put under the 'O' for Opportunity realizing that open discussions of how and why mistakes occur is one of the greatest opportunities for improved customer service.

Make sure your company is capitalizing on your opportunities. Employees and customers will benefit in an environment that realizes we are all human beings, trying our best to get through days that are sometimes difficult.

Your path to customer loyalty may not always be smooth, but if handled correctly, even those bumps in the road may forge a stronger relationship with the most important people in your business...your customers!

CHAPTER TWO

No Excuses Needed

How to Prepare Yourself for Providing Cross-Cultural Customer Service

Tracy Brown

Tracy Brown is President of Person To Person Consulting, a human resources consulting and training firm based in Dallas, Texas. She is the author of the book, *"Breaking the Barrier of Bias"* and four audio programs, including: *"motiVersity™: Motivating While Valuing Diversity"*.

Tracy has designed or delivered diversity training for clients like American Heart Association, The Sabre Group, Dallas Central Appraisal District, American Express and the FAA.

At Parkland Health & Hospital System, the YWCA and City of Dallas, she's conducted customer service training. And when Sky Chefs, Mrs. Bairds Bakeries, and Kaiser Permanente needed external support for Human Resources projects, they called on Person To Person Consulting.

Areas of Expertise:

- Diversity Strategy
- Cross-Cultural Communication Skills
- Team Building
- Assessing and Building Team Trust
- Excellence and Empowerment

Person To Person Consulting
Dallas, TX • 888-316-4447 • www.TracyBrown.com

Tracy Brown

No Excuses Needed

How to Prepare Yourself for Providing Cross-Cultural Customer Service

I could easily title this chapter "Treating Everyone Fairly Does Not Mean Treating Everyone the Same!" I am surprised at the number of people who think that in order to be fair they have to treat everyone the same.

Well that doesn't work. It doesn't work with your family. It doesn't work with your co-workers. And it definitely doesn't work with customers.

Now wait a minute! Some of you are jumping to the conclusion that I'm suggesting you make up individual rules, individual policies and individual sales promotions for each person you come into contact with. Sorry, I don't believe you have to go to that extreme either.

When we talk about valuing diversity or managing diversity in the work environment we are talking about:

- recognizing both the differences and similarities between people
- understanding how individual experiences and cultural norms might affect our relationships with co-workers and customers
- remembering there are many characteristics we can't see when we look at a person that have a big effect on our relationships with co-workers and customers
- learning it can be fun to learn more about what makes people different from ourselves and to share with others those things that make us unique or special

MULTI-CULTURAL CUSTOMERS

So if you can't treat everyone the same, and you can't treat everyone completely differently, how do you provide great service and keep your sanity? It's not easy but it is simple.

To provide excellent customer service to a multi-cultural consumer base you must recognize your biases, create flexibility in response and learn to communicate cross-culturally. Let's look at a real life example.

The Restaurant

It is a very busy night in the restaurant and everyone is working really hard. Luckily you have a great team of friendly servers who get along well and provide good customer service.

David is finishing up his third week of employment, but he had 5 years of restaurant experience before he moved to your city. He's been doing a great job and there have been no complaints about him from co-workers or customers.

You overhear him asking another employee to switch tables with him because he can't stand waiting on those kind of people at the table he's been assigned. He also says, "I can't understand them half the time; and they never give decent tips." He tells the co-worker he'll give him the whole tip from both tables if he'll switch.

Before you can interrupt, you get paged by the hostess who has been at the restaurant since the day it opened. She is one of the best employees and rarely needs any help. When you get to the front of the restaurant you find a couple who have just finished dinner. They want to file a complaint with the manager.

They explain the food was very good, but the service was terrible. They say their server practically ignored them even though he kept checking on the table right across the aisle. They also tell you they were offended when he said something they ordered was the favorite with "you baby boomers."

After you apologize you offer them a gift certificate toward their next meal. But they tell you they don't intend to come back and they'll tell all their friends to stay away as well.

Discussion Starters

1. How do stereotypes and assumptions seem to be affecting service delivery in this restaurant?
2. If you were the team leader on duty what would you say to David? (Taking disciplinary action and referring to policy is not the best answer.)
3. Beyond David, how might you coach the rest of the staff?
4. What are some assumptions or stereotypes employees might have in your organization about different kinds of customers?
5. What are some examples of "everyday" language that might offend your customers – even though the employee didn't mean to be rude?

Dimensions of Diversity

In the book "Workforce America" Loden and Rosener present a model they refer to as "The Dimensions of Diversity" model.

"We will define primary Dimensions of Diversity as those immutable human differences that are inborn and/or that exert an important impact on our early socialization and an ongoing impact throughout our lives. Like interlocking segments of a sphere, they represent the core of our individual identities . . . they shape our basic self-image as well as our fundamental world view."

"Secondary Dimensions of Diversity are those that can be changed. They are mutable differences that we acquire, discard, and/or modify throughout our lives . . . they add contour and breadth to our self-definition."

Dimensions of Diversity are not values or beliefs . . . our values and beliefs are the result of the combination of different dimensions.

The authors identified primary and secondary dimensions as listed below:

Primary Dimensions

- Age
- Race
- Ethnicity
- Sexual Orientation
- Physical Ability
- Gender

Secondary Dimensions

- Geography
- Religion
- Education
- Marital Status
- Parental Status
- Profession
- Income
- Military Experience

Primary Dimensions are characteristics or factors that are "immutable". Generally these are either genetic or a main factor by which people act (or are acted upon). Secondary Dimensions are characteristics or factors that include a significant element of choice. But choice does not refer to behavior; it refers to existence. We all choose our behavior, or the way we respond, to each of the different dimensions.

The most important lesson we can take from the Dimensions of Diversity model is that all of us are affected by many dimensions. And it is important, especially in conflict situations, to recognize the influence of more than one or two of the dimensions.

This is a critical lesson for us to learn and remember because it helps us be less judgmental and more responsive to the needs of our customers. It also helps us reduce our tendency to focus only on the similarities we might share with someone and miss the ways they are different from us which might be important to them.

Recognize Your Biases

When we review the Dimensions of Diversity model it reminds us of all the different elements that helped us form our personal opinions, values, and beliefs. And if we're smart we realize each customer has his or her own set of opinions, values, and beliefs.

If I ask 50 people, "What should you do when you think you have the flu?", I'll get a variety of responses. Each person will basically be sharing his or her biases about what will work. I might agree with some and disagree with others, but none of us are absolutely right or wrong.

Next time you go to the grocery store or to a shopping center, stand to the side and watch people for 15 minutes. You'll notice different styles of communicating. You'll see some people stand very close to the person they are talking to while others need more "space". You'll observe varying patterns related to eye contact and see that nonverbal communication tells you much more than the words people speak.

A bias is a preference; and most of the time our biases are so ingrained in us that we don't even recognize them. Often people use the word bias as if it automatically results in discrimination. But this is not true. A bias is a thought or a feeling. Discrimination requires action.

Discrimination occurs when we allow our biases to control our actions and our actions result in unfair exclusion or disparate treatment of another person.

If you are in a job where you are providing service to customers or clients, it is important for you to be aware of your biases in order to manage them. None of us can completely eliminate our biases, so don't make that your goal. In fact, some of our biases result in us making decisions that protect us or help us excel.

Instead of eliminating all bias, become very conscious of your biases. Then, you will be able to control your behavior and provide excellent service to those clients or customers you might not want to be involved with personally, but who have come to your company to buy your product or use the services offered.

Create Flexibility in Your Responses

Too often we give our customers only one option. We basically tell them, "Do it my way ...or else!" In the long run this backfires on you and on your organization. Adults like having options. Adults don't like to be told what to do. Adults prefer to make choices.

Remember what you think is fair may not be viewed as fair by your customer. Whenever possible provide options. This demonstrates respect for the customer in any situation. But when cross-cultural service is being provided giving clients choices serves to strengthen the relationship and build loyalty for your organization.

LEARN TO COMMUNICATE CROSS-CULTURALLY

There are four basic rules for effective cross-cultural communication:

1. Listen more than you speak
2. Ask open ended questions
3. Suspend judgement
4. Respond to the other person's reality

Listen more than you speak

Often we believe we have communicated because we have spoken. We tell someone what to do or we vocalize our opinion. But we don't listen to the response of the other person. When you focus on listening to your customers you will learn about their expectations and their needs.

Ask open-ended questions

Avoid asking questions that can be answered with "yes" or "no" when communicating with someone who represents a cultural heritage different from your own. Why? By asking questions that require explanations you gain access to more detail. This detailed information can help you understand where the communication breakdown has occurred or it can confirm that the required steps will be followed.

Suspend judgement

This is easier said than done. Most of us want to be right; we equate being right with winning or with being smart. But if you are in a situation where you are providing a service it is more important for you to understand your client's point of view, than to simply get your client to do things your way.

Be aware that your clients may never complain that your services disrespect them. But if you have a competitor who understands your client's cultural norms and offers services that take those norms into consideration, you will lose customers.

Respond to the other person's reality

Often you must deny a request from a client because you are not able to change a policy or an established procedure. However when this happens it is important that you acknowledge the client's view or needs. Instead of saying, "That's wrong," or "That's a stupid way to think," you should affirm the client. You might say, "I understand why you would think that, but here are the two options I can offer you." Or you could say, "I wasn't aware of the problem that could cause. I'll share that information with management. In the meantime, here's what I can do for you."

NEXT STEPS

The primary goal of managing diversity is not to avoid lawsuits, but instead to maximize productivity and to exceed customer expectations. Understanding the law is important, but only as a tool to help you create a work environment that works for all.

What actions will you take to interact effectively with customers representing the diversity in your community?

Check the boxes that apply to you…then add to the list with your own ideas!

- ❑ Go to the websites of my industry's leading professional associations and get an update on the demographics of my customers.
- ❑ Pay attention to the diversity of my customers and consider if they have cultural norms or expectations which are not being met by our current policies or procedures.
- ❑ Lead a discussion with co-workers about diversity to increase awareness.
- ❑ Ask one or more person in my department or organization to teach me more about their cultural background.
- ❑ Share with one or more people in my department or organization things I've never talked about before about my cultural background.
- ❑ Go out of my way to find people from different ethnic groups, age groups and social groups to interact with.
- ❑ Read one article or book each month on diversity-related topics.
- ❑ Pay extra attention to how I define job requirements and notice if I describe the "best qualified" candidate based on (a) skills or (b) cultural comfort.
- ❑ Identify the 2 or 3 dimensions of diversity which most affect the success of my organization and commit to paying attention to those factors -- both with co-workers and with customers.
- ❑ Read the company policies on sexual harassment and equal employment opportunity and ask questions about anything I don't understand.
- ❑ Evaluate my readiness and effectiveness with customers who have disabilities. Be prepared to serve customers who are blind, hearing impaired or using a wheel chair.
- ❑ ______________________________
  ____
  ____
- ❑ ______________________________
  ____
  ____

Treating everyone fairly doesn't mean treating everyone the same. And treating everyone the way you wish to be treated doesn't work if your customer has different norms related to communication, decision-making, body language and other nonverbal signals. Stay alert to expectations and needs expressed by your clients. Most of the time you will be able to stay within policy and still accommodate your clients' needs and expectations.

Look for opportunities to practice cross-cultural customer service and you'll find it's not as difficult as you might have thought. No excuses are needed when you exceed your customers' expectations time and time again!

CHAPTER THREE

WOW Your Customers!

The Roadmap to Exceptional Customer Service and Higher Profits

Regina Clark

Regina M. Clark, a professional speaker, trainer and author is founder of Clark Training & Development. Regina delivers over 100 speaking and training programs a year with an emphasis on Managing Change, Thrilling Customers, Developing Dynamic Presentation Skills and Training FUNdamentals. Regina helps people learn faster, work smarter, and laugh harder.

Regina's background includes over sixteen years in Training & Organizational Development. She has coached CEO's, government officials, hundreds of Six Sigma engineers, educators and business leaders in the art and science of effective communication.

Her clients include Johnson & Johnson, Cummins Engine Company, CIT and other Fortune 500 organizations. Regina is a member of the National Speakers Association, Orange County Chamber of Commerce, and past president of Toastmasters. She is the author of an upcoming book, *You've Got to Keep Your Sense of Humor: Strategies for Balancing Career & Family.*

Clark Training & Development
Goshen, NY • 845-294-7089 • clarktrain@aol.com

Regina Clark

WOW Your Customers!

The Roadmap to Exceptional Customer Service and Higher Profits

Businesses come and go. Today, there is a great deal of competition. Most organizations are fighting for market share. You can shop at Home Depot, Lowe's or the local hardware store. You can purchase gas at Exxon, Mobil, Hess or Gulf. You can use Staples, Kinko's, Office Max or the local printer for your business needs. You can vacation at Walt Disney World in Orlando, Florida or visit Universal Studios and Sea World. You can stay at the Wyndam or the Doubletree. To stay in business and keep your customers coming back, you must WOW them with exceptional customer service. If you don't, someone else will.

Creating WOW experiences for your customers will:

- Improve your reputation
- Increase revenues
- Improve productivity
- Get faster results
- Improve morale

A few years ago, I lost a small gold police badge pendant in a Home Depot store. The pendant had my husband's badge number engraved on it. The store manager told an employee to locate the pendant owner by contacting the New York City Police Department. Because there are over 30,000 police officers in New York City, it took three days for the Home Depot associate to find the precinct phone number and eventually find me. I was thrilled to get the pendant back and I was amazed that the Home Depot store manager cared so much. What a WOW! Today, I am a loyal Home Depot customer.

Exceptional customer service doesn't happen by accident. The secret is simple: identify what it takes to WOW your customers, hire the right people and then exceed the expectations of your customers. All this takes planning.

THE CUSTOMER SERVICE ROADMAP

Think of customer service as a process with inputs and outputs. You need to be actively involved in the process. You can't leave customer service to chance. The roadmap to exceptional customer services has five steps:

- Identify your customers
- Hire the right people
- Determine what it would take to WOW your customers
- Implement the WOW ideas
- Measure the results

IDENTIFY YOUR CUSTOMERS

Before you can WOW the customer, you must understand who the customer is. Your first priority is to identify your customer. You also need to understand that there are two types of customers – internal and external. The external customer is easy to recognize. They are the ones that purchase your product or service. They are the patron at a gas station, the mother purchasing shoes at a shoe outlet and the salesperson buying her client lunch. They are all external customers.

Find out as much as you can about your customers. Do they speak English as a second language? How old are they? Do they shop on line? Do they understand the industry, the service and/or the product? Are they fussy? Are they demanding? Are they wealthy or financially strapped? Do they have time constraints? Are their hands tied due to regulations?

In addition, think about the internal customers who support the people that deal with the external customers. For example, if you work for an organization, the internal customers are your co-workers. Your co-workers rely on you for accurate, timely information. They rely on your experience and expertise. They expect you to treat them with the same respect that you would give an external customer. Why should you care about your internal customers? Without internal customers, you wouldn't be able to support any external customers.

HIRE CUSTOMER FOCUSED EMPLOYEES

Once you understand your customers, you can hire people that will be able to effectively interact with your customers. Customers from all over the world shop at the New York Giorgio Armani store. Giorgio Armani needs to be able to service the customers. They hire salespeople that can speak a variety of languages. When all other things are equal, the essential ingredient in creating a WOW experience is the creative, caring employee that has exceptional interpersonal communication skills. Great communicators are focused on the following areas:

What they say

Use positive, simple language.
Positive: I'll transfer you to Mary, who will be able to help you.
Negative: That's not my job.
Positive: We will get you the part by Friday; it's on back order.
Negative: We don't have the part.
Positive: I'll give you an answer by 3:00PM today.
Negative: I don't have time to think about your request.

At the Ritz-Carlton luxury hotel, employees are told never to say "Hi, OK or folks." A proper greeting would be "Good morning, good evening or welcome."

What they look like when they communicate

- Smile at the customers
- Make eye contact
- Stand up straight
- Maintain a neat, clean, professional, appropriate appearance
- Limit or avoid body piercing
- Use open gestures
- Greet the customers appropriately
- A firm handshake and a polite introduction when dealing with external customers

How they sound

- Use appropriate sounds and tones
- Volume, rate, pitch, articulation and resonance impact a person's ability to sound professional
- Never yell at a customer

Are they actively listening?

- Try to put yourself in the other person's circumstances
- Listen with empathy
- Focus on the speaker when you are listening
- Don't interrupt the speaker

Hiring the right people, those who are already focused on customer service, is the best way to ensure WOW experiences for your clients. When you are interviewing job candidates, get the interviewee to give you specific information. Theoretical answers aren't very helpful in assessing job candidates. Anyone can tell you that they like working with people. You need specific examples. Past performance is the best indicator of future behavior. Here are some sample questions to guide the interview:

- Describe your experience working with customers.
- Tell me about a time when you had to deal with a difficult customer. What exactly did you do?
- Tell me about a time when you thrilled a customer.
- Tell me about a time when you had to break or bend a rule to satisfy a customer.
- Tell me about a time when you failed to satisfy a customer.
- Give me an example of positive feedback that you received from a customer.

IDENTIFYING CUSTOMER EXPECTATIONS

Customers expect a lot, especially if they are handing over their hard-earned dollars for a service or product. Sometimes the expectation is linked to the cost. Imagine a person checking into a Holiday Inn. The person expects a clean, safe hotel with a friendly staff at a reasonable rate. The same person checks into a Ritz-Carlton luxury hotel a week later. The expectations are different. A clean, safe hotel is not enough; the person now expects a luxurious hotel, with gourmet food, and exceptional service. The Ritz-Carlton hotel chain prides itself in providing exceptional customer service. The customer also pays for the service. The first time I stayed at a Ritz-Carlton hotel in San Francisco, I felt like a princess, everyone was so polite and gracious! WOW! Now I expect that level of service from the Ritz-Carlton. The next time I stay at a Ritz-Carlton, it will be harder to WOW me because I expect so much. Before you can create a WOW, you must figure out what customers expect.

Take a moment to think about your customers. What do they expect from you, your product, and your organization? Are you giving your customers what they expect? Are you meeting their expectations or are you WOWing them? A WOWed customer will come back!

Find out if you are meeting your customers' expectations. If you're not sure, ask your customers. Use focus groups, interviews or surveys. If you're not meeting customer expectations, you're not doing a good job running your business. Are there obstacles that prevent you from providing great service? If there are, get rid of the obstacles!

Let's look at an organization that is ambivalent towards customer service, the New York City Department of Motor Vehicles. Most people in New York City do not look forward to visiting the Department of Motor Vehicles. I have lived in New York for over 40 years and have never heard of anyone talking about exceptional customer service at the NYC DMV. To tell you the truth, people dread going to the DMV.

What does the customer expect?

- Long lines
- To be in the wrong line the first time
- Rude service
- Aggravation
- Frustration
- Confusing signs
- Lack of available help

How can the Department of Motor Vehicles WOW (thrill, delight) customers?

- Shorten the lines
- Hire friendly, customer focused employees that want to service customers
- Hire a greeter or customer service representative to answer questions
- Hand out free black pens

It wouldn't be difficult for the NYC DMV to WOW customers but without a business reason to do so, they probably won't bother. There is no competition for the customers business. Can you take the same chance with your customers?

What do customers expect from a hospital? Here, the external customer could be the patient, the patient's family, the patient's visitors or someone in the community. Most people do not look forward to a hospital stay. Most dread it. In addition, hospitals are focused on patient care; they go through strict joint commission audits in order to stay accredited. Some hospitals are beginning to think about the patient as a customer with choices.

What does the healthcare customer expect?

- Clean, sanitary environment
- Safe environment
- Up to date equipment
- Knowledgeable, trained, certified, caring staff
- Medical experts
- Timely treatment
- Accurate treatment (the right medication, the right diagnosis, the right procedure)
- Pleasant workers
- Mediocre food

Would it be difficult for a local hospital to WOW customers? Not really, providing great food and a free phone might WOW some customers. Is it worthwhile for a local hospital to WOW customers? Absolutely. Patients have choices when it comes to hospital stays. Hospitals need to fill beds to stay in business.

I have worked with hospitals that are having a hard time just meeting patient expectations because of reductions in staffing. The medical staff wants to provide exceptional care but due to time constraints, they cannot spend as much time with their patients as they would like. A few years ago, I sat in a hospital room for hours with my Dad. He had just gotten out of surgery. No one came into the room for over three hours. He didn't even have a pitcher of water at his bedside. Imagine being in the same situation without a family member to assist you. The medical procedure went well but the post op care was seriously lacking. I will never consider that hospital for a procedure again. When customers aren't satisfied, they don't return for another disappointing experience. Further, most will tell their friends about the bad service causing even more damage to your reputation and your business.

IS MEETING EXPECTATIONS GOOD ENOUGH?

When you meet customer expectations, you are doing your job. We expect doctors and nurses in hospitals to take good care of us, that is their job. We might not expect a doctor to spend 45 minutes by our bedside describing a procedure. We might not expect a doctor to call us at home a week later to check on us. When doctors go above and beyond what we expect, they are creating a WOW experience for us. When you exceed customer expectations, you are going above and beyond your job description and creating a WOW for your customers!

Let's look at one last example. What does the customer expect from a luxury retail store?

- Quality merchandise
- Personal service
- Private dressing room
- A knowledgeable salesperson
- Fashionable merchandise
- To feel excited about the product

A few years ago, I interviewed one of the top saleswomen at Giorgio Armani. She shared some of her secrets with me. She keeps a very detailed client book. She knows about her clients, her clients' families, her clients' likes and dislikes. She spends hours every night on handwritten personal correspondence. She anticipates what her clients will need for future engagements and then sends samples to their home so that they can try on the clothing at their leisure. She takes great pride in her wrapping and packaging of merchandise. She sends her clients gifts – fresh flowers, candy, etc. She is an exceptional saleswoman and amazingly creative. Her personal appearance is exquisite. She represents Giorgio Armani beautifully. She creates WOW experiences every day for her clients. She is also a fabulous role model for other Giorgio Armani salespeople.

THE WOW EXPERIENCE

During the past fifteen years, I have listened to hundreds of people talk about the WOW experience. The one thing every WOW experience has in common is an exceptional, thoughtful human being. The Home Depot manager realized that my pendant might have sentimental value. The Ritz-Carlton hotel in San Francisco is a beautiful luxury hotel, but the WOW came from the waiters, waitresses, doormen, front desk staff and maids that I encountered. Horst Schulze, president of the Ritz-Carlton, is one of the few hotel presidents that takes an active role in training hotel associates about customer service. His obsession with quality service has made the luxury hotel chain the only service company that's a two-time winner of the Commerce Department's Malcolm Baldridge National Quality Award. Successful salespeople know that you always under promise and over deliver.

Making the WOW last: Measure the results

Once an organization has a reputation for delivering exceptional service, the challenge becomes keeping the reputation alive. Are the customers still thrilled after all these years? If Walt Disney stopped creating and inventing after the Magic Kingdom was built, what would you think about Walt Disney today? Fortunately, under the leadership of Michael Eisner, Disney is always reinventing itself with new hotels, new theme parks, new movies and new products. You can visit Disney in Orlando, Florida and have a different experience every time. Continually check and re-check what your customers think about your service.

CHAPTER FOUR

Taming Those Tigers!

Dealing With Difficult & Demanding People

Rebecca "Tiger" Harrison

In a recent interview, Tom Brightbill, talk show host, nicknamed Rebecca Harrison "The Queen of the Customer Service Jungle."

Dubbed "Tiger" by her worst heckler, Rebecca is passionate about "Taming the Tigers" and "Dealing with Difficult and Demanding People." With a background as a radio personality, a staff writer with a metropolitan newspaper and a sales professional, Tiger's entrepreneurial spirit has lead her to 100 speaking engagements throughout the U.S. and Canada last year.

This year "Tiger" Harrison celebrates her 9th year as R. S. Harrison International, a speaking and training organization focused on adding value to businesses through training people to value people.

Tiger received a BA in Mass Communication and Marketing from both California Polytechnic University in San Luis Obispo, CA, and California State University at Hayward, CA.

Tiger is an accredited member of The National Speakers Association, The American Society of Training and Development. AT&T named her as part of their Diamond Award Winning Team for Human Resource Role Model Excellence. Her company is verified as a Minority Woman Business Enterprise.

R. S. Harrison International
San Ramon, CA • 925-798-4751 • www.TigerTalk.com

Rebecca "Tiger" Harrison

Taming Those Tigers!

Dealing With Difficult & Demanding People

Do you work with difficult people? Live with demanding people? Or are you sometimes the difficult and demanding person? Dealing with difficult people is...well difficult!

Difficult, demanding, and irate behaviors test the skills of our best service providers. Most often, service professionals do not receive an instruction book. Usually, we learn by trial, error, and being on the firing line.

THE FIRING LINE

One late night at Dallas-Fort Worth International Airport, a sharply dressed man approached the gate agent. Based on his appearance, he was the CEO of some Fortune 500 company. The ticket agent explained the flight was delayed. The "CEO" raised his voice sharing his frustration with the rest of the airport. He was IRATE! His choice of words was shocking, and had such a rhythm they almost sounded poetic. The agent turned red, but remained silent. Stunned and speechless, she handed him his boarding pass. Moments later the plane began boarding. The "CEO" pushed his way into line, a cell phone stuck in his ear. As he presented his boarding pass, an arm reached out and grabbed his. It was the agent's supervisor. "Excuse me sir, this will only take a moment." "I don't have a moment! I'm in a hurry!" the "CEO" stated. "Sir, are you aware that I can stop you from boarding this plane?" "What are you talking about!" retorted the "CEO". "The language you used with our agent was inappropriate and abusive. I'd like to ask you to apologize before you board."

STAND BEHIND YOUR FRONT LINE

Although a manager's overall view is the company's market and customers, his focus is on the "Internal" Customer as well, because they service the "External" Customer. When this is the managerial focus, the level of service provided by his front line will increase.

Customers can be more demanding and difficult than ever before. They expect instant gratification. "Air Rage", "Road Rage", and "Cubical Wars" have become everyday phrases and situations that staff deals with daily.

In her book *Take Your Life Back*, Odette Pollar says: "Our work week has expanded by a full day and we have 37% less leisure time than 25 years ago." To increase motivation and productivity of our staff, we need to give our people the tools they need to meet the increased demand of more work and less leisure.

What policies does your organization have for dealing with abusive customers? What action is your staff allowed to take? Do you train them how to implement these actions? Would your supervisors stand behind the agent, like the supervisor at the Dallas-Fort Worth Airport?

Stand Behind Your Front Line!

The passenger standing behind "the Sharply Dressed Man", was me. Before boarding the plane, I watched the supervisor debrief the situation with his agent. By the actions he had taken with the customer, he had shifted his agent from being shocked to feeling supported. Together they reviewed the situation: her actions, tone of voice, eye contact and body language. The supervisor pointed out that the customer's reaction was not due to something she had done or not done; this customer was having a bad day. He recommended she go outside for an unscheduled break and some fresh air.

In a study conducted by one of our call center clients, unscheduled breaks increased productivity from 6.15 hours per day to 6.85 in a 12-month period. And, according to a study by W. B. Cannon at Harvard University over a hundred years ago, it only takes two minutes to reverse the body's chemical response to "Fight or Flight".

A short break allows an employee to refocus and release stress so they will be able to continue to meet company service standards.

TOOLS FOR DEALING WITH DIFFICULT & DEMANDING CUSTOMERS

1. Have written polices for dealing with difficult and demanding customers
2. Train your staff on these policies
3. Stand behind your front line by taking action
4. Debrief after a difficult situation
5. Then give the employee a short break

10 Reasons Customers Become Difficult & Demanding

We recently conducted an internet survey on customer service complaints. The overwhelming response crashed our web site repeatedly. In the survey, three questions were asked:

- What is your worse customer service nightmare?
- Why?
- What needs to be different to make you happy?

Over 3700 irate customers from Russia, the Ukraine, China, Panama, Puerto Rico, Canada and throughout the United States responded. Fortune 100 Companies, medium and small businesses were the target of customer complaints. Almost no industry was left untouched. Respondents were clear about what companies are not doing to meet their customer service expectations.

The survey found these Top 10 Reasons Customers Become Irate with service providers:

1. The Customer is Having a Bad Day
2. The Customer is Greeted with an Uncaring or Indifferent Attitude
3. Poor Response Time, On Hold Forever (more than 30 sec.)
4. The Customer Felt They Were Not Listened To
5. Service Representative Did Not Take Responsibility
6. Service Representative Says One Thing, Does Another
7. The Customer Had a Bad Experience with You Before
8. The Company Did Not Stand Behind a Guarantee
9. The Service Representative Did Not Follow Through
10. The Service Representative Showed a Lack of Knowledge of Product or Service

THE T.A.M.E. PRINCIPLE: TOOLS FOR DEALING WITH DIFFICULT BEHAVIORS

T- TAKE Ownership

It pays to apologize for our customer's frustration in a service situation. What does it cost? Ego. When was the last time you were stuck in an ego tug-a-war? Would you be willing to let go of your need to be right...if it saved you time, energy and money?

Tool: "You Could Be Right®"

"Could" is the operative word in this phrase. Would you not agree that almost anything is possible? Is this condescending? That is not the intention. This is simply a communication tool to handle the constant demands of our customers.

Benefits:

- The customer feels in control
- The customer feels they have won

AND

- It takes less time and energy
- It begins to diffuse the situation

Example:

External Customer: "I need to get on the plane. I don't know what you're talking about. Your agent's the one with the problem!"

Response: "You Could Be Right® "(Pause)...our agents deal with a lot of difficult customers and sometimes they do lose their patience. However, we observed your interaction with our agent and we feel you were out of line. We're asking you to apologize before boarding...

Example:

Internal Customer: "I'm always the one picking up the slack around here. It's not my responsibility and it's not fair!"

Response: "You Could Be Right®" (Pause)...We want to hear what you have to say. Right now I'm in a time crunch.How about tomorrow at 5:00?... or Wednesday morning? (Pause)...Will you prepare a summary of your duties for us to look over?"

A - ASK Questions Vs. "Telling"

As managers, we know it works best to let the lesson be the teacher not us. Let's pick up on our "internal customer" example above.

Questions to Ask:

- "Let us take a look at what you prepared...What do you think is a fair solution?" - Marla Winitz, President, HR in A Box.
- "What can I do to increase your enjoyment and growth here?"
- "If I'm willing to do this, what are you willing to do to be part of the solution?"

Questions vs. making statements opens the lines of communication even in the most difficult situations.

M - ME The Most Important Word to Our Customer

Tools:

- Use "We" in place of "I" to build a united front and develop consensus
- Let the customer find the solution (usually they ask for less than we would be willing to give).

People wear two signs around their neck:

1. "Do You Know Who I AM?"
2. "Why Should I?"

1st Sign: "Do You Know Who I Am?"

Responses:

"Your business is our business" - Traci Bild, President, Dynamic Productions.

"If you've gotten the impression that your business doesn't matter, let me apologize."

2nd Sign: "Why Should I?"

Concept: Both our internal and external customers need to see their personal benefit. They are not being difficult. It is just human nature.

E - Entitlement

When we turn those difficult customers around, we form a bond of loyalty like no other. They will stick with us like super glue. Not only do we earn their business; they will bring us more...if we "Ask".

Asking: "Who do you know who'd be interested in our service/products? AND What else can we do to support your professional growth? We know any relationship works best when it's a two way street and we appreciate your support."

The first part of this phrase comes from network marketing genius Mary Kay Ash, Chairwoman Emeritus, Mary Kay Cosmetics.

The phrase following "AND" is the part that is usually left out. This is a key when asking for referrals. Everyone is overwhelmed with demands on their time. The personal benefit to referring us needs to be verbalized.

WHY CUSTOMERS LEAVE

A challenge for any organization in upgrading their service to the next level is developing and maintaining a company vision that is customer focused. Vision always begins with senior management and filters down to the front line.

A recent survey by U.S. News & World Report illustrated how crucial attitude is to a company's service success. There were six reasons why customers leave, and more than 50% of the total were due to only one of those reasons, while only two of the reasons made up 82% of the responses. What are the two reasons?

Why Customers Leave

68% Because of an indifferent/uncaring attitude by company employees
14% Dissatisfied by the service or product
9% Buy from competitors
5% Influenced by a bad experience of a friend
3% Move away
1% Die

WHAT DIFFICULT & DEMANDING PEOPLE WANT

Research has shown that the average U.S. company loses 20% of its customers annually. In most cases, loss of customers can be traced back to the dissatisfaction.

Unfortunately, most dissatisfied customers do not even bother to complain. Customer service complaints can be golden opportunities to develop loyal customers and increase business.

Many times customer dissatisfaction can be as simple as the little things. "It's the little things--like saying 'How can I help You' that makes the difference with customers", says John Brennan, HR VP, WindRiver Systems, Inc.

Dealing with difficult and dissatisfied customers, and doing the little things is everyones responsibility. That is why it is so important to see that everyone is onboard.

GET EVERYONE ON THE SAME PAGE

The "Service Matrix", taught by Jerry Twentyman the President of Electromotion.com, is a good exercise to use for lunchtime training with your employees. It is one way to start shifting your organization's focus to the real needs of today's global customers.

The Exercise

Take out a piece of paper. Draw a square. Divide the square into four equal squares. On one axis write "Technical" and on the other axis write "Non-Technical." "Non-Technical" refers to service.

Now label each axis of the large square into two equal parts: "Good" and "Average"

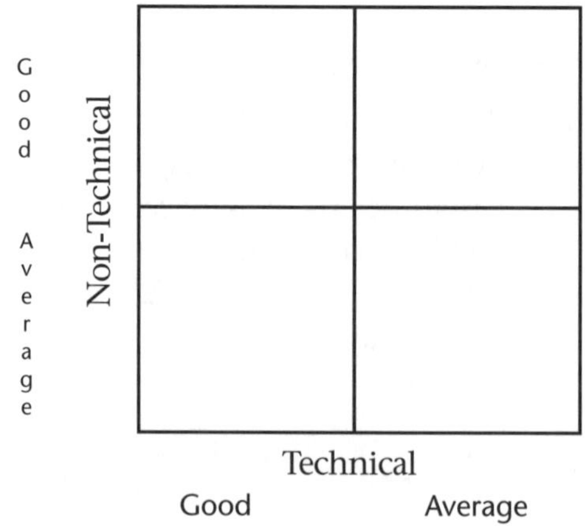

"Service Matrix" (2)

Let's start with the two most obvious boxes. First, the top left box: If you do a good job technically and a good job non-technically - You win. Draw a $ sign in the top left box.

Next, the lower right box: If your technical delivery is average, and your non-technical service is average, your customer is disappointed: usually you lose their business. Write "Lose" in the lower right box.

The last two boxes are where it becomes interesting. Start with the top right box. If your technical delivery is average and your non-technical service is good you still win. Draw a $ sign in the top right box.

Finally, the lower left box - If your technical delivery is good (even on the level of genius) and your non-technical delivery is average you "Lose". Write "Lose" in this box.

The Service Matrix illustrates the benefit of changing the way we value customers…it changes the value of our businesses. People relate to people, not process.

"The moral of the story is, you can be the hottest tech around and lose every time." - Michael Price, President of Michael Price Associates, a computing company in Silicon Valley.

Ask yourself: "What can I do to make every service situation less frustrating and more rewarding for my internal and external customers?"

CHAPTER FIVE

How Attitude Impacts Customer Service

In Business, There's Always Someone Watching

Carl Herrick

Energetic, experienced and exciting are several of the descriptions attendees write virtually every week following the successful conclusion to the more than 150 half and full-day workshops led annually by this dynamic corporate trainer and speaker. With over 20 years of outstanding performance in the fields of engineering, sales and speaking, he steps up to the plate each day with the skills and desire needed to hit the ball out of the park, and ready to show your employees how to do the same.

Well over 10,000 individuals seeking to improve their skills in customer service, selling, communication, product knowledge and retailing have attended his workshops and seminars during just the past five years. Voting with their wallets and pens clients have come back time and again, scoring his efforts at an incredible 4.96 evaluation on a scale of 1-5.00. Over $25,000,000 in direct sales to Fortune 500 companies combined with a customer retention rate in excess of 97% during his career make him the perfect speaker to assist your company in achieving the highest customer satisfaction and loyalty scores in your industry.

Herrick Consulting Group
Ponchatoula, La • 985-386-2263 • herrick@i-55.com

Carl Herrick

How Attitude Impacts Customer Service

In Business, There's Always Someone Watching

Every time an employee interacts with a customer, the opportunity exists for a report card to be created. And it's the employee's responsibility to achieve a high grade.

In the '80s the president of Scandinavian Airlines System (SAS), Mr. Jan Carlzon, called such interactions "Moments of Truth." He defined them as "any event in which the customer comes into contact with any aspect of the organization and gets an impression of the quality of the organization's services." Of themselves these moments are neither positive nor negative. But the customer's rating of them will make or break your company.

At the former Chrysler Corporation (now DaimlerChrysler), which had as its logo a five pointed star called Pentastar, these opportunities were called "Star Moments." When the outcome was positive for the customer, it was called a "Shining Star Moment." If the outcome was negative (and therefore also negative for Chrysler) it was labeled a "Falling Star Moment."

During the nineties Chrysler spent millions of dollars creating and facilitating training to teach this concept in a program called "Customer One." Before it ended, the program trained tens of thousands of corporate and dealer personnel around the country and the world how to regularly achieve "Shining Star Moments." The goal was to improve relationships with its existing and potential customers, both external and internal, by encouraging employees to regard customers with greater levels of respect and gratitude than had previously been demonstrated. By all accounts, the program was a major success.

In fact it's probably not coincidence that in 1996, within 18 months after the multi-year program was completed, Forbes magazine selected Chrysler as its Company of the Year. I still receive inquiries today seeking to learn if the program can be re-established. Without question, having employees focused on excellent customer service improves a company's bottom line.

To emphasize the control employees have over "moments of truth" I sometimes use the following demonstration. I hold up a $20 bill, and ask the class "if I give one of you this money to purchase dinner for someone in need, is the $20 bill good or bad?" The class always replies "the bill is good." Next, I tell them I will give someone the $20 bill if they will pour the full pitcher of ice water sitting on their table over the head of a fellow student. Usually the class laughs and quickly agrees that in the second scenario the payment of $20 would be bad. It is then very easy for me to gain agreement that the $20 bill of itself is neither good nor bad. But what we choose to do with it is a different story.

Similarly, interactions with customers and clients are of themselves neither good nor bad. But how we control our actions during these moments greatly impacts whether the interactions are seen as positive or negative.

ASK NOT WHAT YOUR COMPANY CAN DO FOR YOU

You've probably heard the saying, "It's not your aptitude but your gratitude that determines your altitude." Having a natural talent for something really helps you get ahead, but combining it with a great attitude moves you to new heights in virtually every line of work.

Most of us do provide excellent service at least part of the time. The challenge, however, lies in maintaining a positive attitude day in and day out, through good times and bad. On the days when you wonder why you even got out of bed, what is it that allows you to still provide good or even great customer service?

What's worked best for me is taking a minute to focus on being thankful. For my health, my family, my job, career, the United States or anything else I can think of. On many occasions when I was physically, mentally or emotionally exhausted but still had customers to serve, I've let my mind open to see around me other people who serve each day. Many have low-paying jobs at restaurants, stores and dozens of other small businesses that can be found in every community. Often times they work at least as hard as I do, for less pay, fewer perks and less recognition. It isn't hard for me to know how hard they work because at different times I've been a janitor, waiter, and ditch digger.

I joke with friends and clients that one of the best things that happened to me was a summer spent digging through the rocky soil of New England. During my next semester at college studying didn't seem like such a bad deal.

By taking the focus off ourselves, we're able to create feelings of gratitude that lift our spirits and provide renewed enthusiasm for assisting everyone we come in contact with. Many times this strategy has bailed me out and allowed me to go from mediocre to excellent effort and customer service.

For me the aptitude, attitude, altitude saying has now been transformed into, "It's not your attitude but your gratitude that determines your altitude."

ENTHUSIASM SHOWS, SO DOES APATHY

I recently visited a local McDonald's restaurant for breakfast. It's a relatively new store so the building is in great shape, the furnishings are new and I can imagine anyone employed there would be able to have a feeling of pride in its appearance. As I prepared to leave I collected my trash, stood up and began to walk with my tray toward one of the cabinets McDonalds provides. One of the workers, a woman probably in her early 20's, had just picked a stack of trays off the top of the cabinet. Seconds later, when I tried to place my trash inside the cabinet I noticed it was turned sideways. I placed my tray on top, easily rotated the cabinet (which was on casters) to the correct position, threw away my trash and left. But I couldn't help wondering why the young woman hadn't rotated the cabinet herself. The reason could be as simple as that she didn't notice, or as potentially troubling as she couldn't be bothered. Failing to turn around a trash cabinet may seem trivial, but is it? Or could performance like this at your workplace be the tip of an iceberg trying to sink your company's morale and profits?

I know what Skip Bertman, legendary Louisiana State University baseball coach, would say. After taking over a second rate program in the mid '80s he transformed the "Fighting" Tigers into the team of the decade in the '90s, leading LSU to an amazing six College World Series Championships between 1989 and 2000. To hear him tell it, a key to their success was taking ownership of not only the field of play but the stadium itself. With little, if any, fan and alumni support, Skip never dreamed of asking for funds to fix up the below par stadium he'd inherited. Instead, he and his players literally began work repairing backstop netting, painting dugouts and cleaning up restrooms and concession stands.

The result was increased pride, in not only their playing skills, but also in their "home." Coach Bertman understands that his team provides entertainment for the fans, and anything he and his players can do to make the fans more comfortable is a good idea. In turn the fans support and excite him and his players and...well, you get the picture. To this day, Skip says he wants to know how the hot dogs taste and how long the concession stand lines are. If everything isn't great, let's work on it until we get it right.

SALES PEOPLE SELL...SALESPROS SERVE

Most of my work career has revolved around selling products and services, or teaching others how to do so, though I actually graduated with a degree in engineering, and worked as a shipboard engineer for three years before migrating into sales.

Fortunately for me, that transition meant I was hired by the Xerox Corporation to work with a group of very bright and ethical managers and sales consultants who believed as I do in serving the client in every way possible. Excellent training was provided. The focus was placed on what was called "needs analysis." We were taught to learn our products, listen closely for client needs and recommend the best way to address those needs. Emphasis was placed on professionalism and in having faith that our products combined with our hard work would be attractive enough to win us the client's business and keep it. And it did! Working in this kind of environment felt natural to me, as it still does today.

Too often, especially in a sales environment (and what company doesn't want every employee to help "sell" its products), the emphasis is too strong on selling and not strong enough on serving. When this happens, management usually resorts to techniques instead of principles, with the result being manipulation instead of motivation. Employees are manipulated to pressure customers and customers are manipulated to purchase products and services they may not need, won't benefit from or paid too much for. The reason this happens so often is that it works for a little while. So, mediocre or unscrupulous managers continue to employ these techniques. But sooner or later the customers find out and resent it. When this happens, the client relationship is lost.

Another down side is that good sales people, who sincerely want to help their customers and who have integrity and ethics, soon become discouraged or adopt a "bad attitude" and their internal image and job performance trail off. Before long they end up leaving. The result is that the customer, the employee and the employer all lose.

GREAT CUSTOMER SERVICE = LOYALTY = MONEY, REAL MONEY

In his book "The Loyalty Effect," author Frederick Reichheld emphasizes what's at stake regarding good customer service. His studies determined that "an increase in customer retention of 5% can result in a 100% increase in profits." They also show that retaining 2% more of your existing customers can provide savings equal to a 10% reduction in operating costs. In a position I held with an engineering and consulting company we managed to keep virtually every customer in my territory during a four-year period, and add additional business through referrals and new accounts. The result was an increase in revenue from $600,000 a year to just over $4,000,000. Needless to say, our profits at these accounts climbed as revenues increased, while operating costs as a percentage of revenue decreased. And the best part was I was able to establish strong relationships with my clients and can truly say it was fun going to work in the morning. I saw myself not as merely a "sales consultant" but as a virtual partner. The customers embraced this mentality as well and win/win situations became so common as to be totally expected.

In fact, one morning as I walked through a maintenance shop

wearing my bright blue company hardhat I was stopped by one of the client's foreman. He and I had worked together on several projects. He had a quizzical look on his face as he asked, "What are you doing wearing that hardhat?" I was surprised by his question and replied, "What hardhat should I be wearing?" He then asked me "where's your "company hat"." Suddenly I realized that for some time he had thought I was a co-worker, not a contractor. I thanked him for making my day.

Having a great attitude really paid off at that account. I had been the account manager for this client for several years when one day the head of purchasing called. He invited us to attend a cocktail party honoring the top thirty vendors whom they purchased products and services from. My area manager and I were thrilled to learn the client had initiated a "Partner's In Excellence" quality awards program (without telling us) and selected thirty vendors as the best out of 3000. We were really blown away when during the reception they further announced that only three companies, including us, had received an even higher award, being selected as the top three out of 3000!

Two years later I moved into a different field of engineering, but serving the same industries. This same customer was more than happy to continue the relationship with me and within a year became my single largest account, spending more than $1 million in a 12-month period. Like I said, great service = loyalty = money, real money.

25 STEPS TO GREAT CUSTOMER SERVICE

Smart companies, who want to excel at customer service, teach their entire workforce to focus on the following:

1. Focus on serving first, selling second!
2. Learn about your company's products, services and the industry(s) it serves
3. Take the attitude of not just getting the client's business, but earning it!

4. Be aggressive, but not abusive. Customers (and bosses) like to see initiative
5. Communicate solutions, not just problems
6. Learn, remember and use the customer's name as often as possible
7. Be considerate of the customer's time as well as their money
8. Clearly communicate product and service commitments to avoid having the customer set false expectations that probably won't be met
9. Be willing to fight for, not with your customers
10. Think of yourself as developing a career, not merely working at a job. It increases your enthusiasm and energy level
11. Be confident, but not lead by false pride. Understand it takes a team effort
12. Take ownership of your responsibilities and understand the important role you play as a part of the company
13. Believe you personally positively affect your company's image
14. At all times show respect for every customer, both external and internal
15. See every contact as a potential "customer for life," not a one time transaction and remember (especially if you're in sales), "You can shear a sheep every year, but you can only skin it once."
16. See workplace difficulties as opportunities for personal growth
17. Keep an open mind. Be flexible and adaptable to client and employer needs
18. Have the courage to take on new challenges and responsibilities

19. Be coachable. Seek to improve existing skills and learn new ones
20. Be dependable. Failure to keep simple promises is a common reason given by customers for dissatisfaction
21. Pay attention to detail. It shows the customers they're important to you
22. Come to work rested and ready to serve
23. Overlook honest mistakes by customers and co-workers
24. Make an effort to learn your customer's business. Work to become a valuable partner when possible. Their success makes yours more likely
25. Make it easy for them to remember your name. Name recognition breeds comfort and strengthens relationships. Share it, and wear it when appropriate.

CHAPTER SIX

First Impression...Lasting Impression

How to Create Instant Rapport and Build Strong Customer Relationships

Jana L. High

Jana High is an author as well as a full-of-energy seminar leader and keynote speaker! Jana's presentations are delivered with an enthusiastic and dynamic speaking style. Coupled with her ability to teach "usable" techniques for problem solving, Jana simply captivates her audiences.

In addition to serving as an adjunct instructor at Southern Methodist University, Jana has designed and delivered seminars, keynotes, and training for major corporations and organizations, including NCR, American Express, The Associates, Accenture, Perot Systems, Mobil Oil, Hunt Oil, Bank One, Southwestern Bell, Farmers Insurance, The National Ice Cream and Yogurt Association to name a few.

As a highly sought after keynote presenter, Jana's incredible story of "Petting the Dolphin" demonstrates her belief that you have to take RISKS and embrace your CHALLENGES to be successful. Her keynote presentations are delivered with humor, high-energy, enthusiasm, and are touching, motivational and inspiring. They will exhilarate and entertain audiences to encourage them to believe they can achieve their greatest dreams.

JLH Presentations
Plano, TX • 866-820-6303 • www.jlhpresentations.com

Jana L. High

First Impression...Lasting Impression

How to Create Instant Rapport and Build Strong Customer Relationships

"Don't slouch." "Are you going to wear that?" "Your hair is a mess." At the risk of sounding like your mother, this is good advice. In fact, the old saying that "you never get a second chance to make a first impression" is true.

Why are first impressions so important? Several studies show that we all make numerous and lasting assessments of a person within the first few seconds of meeting. These assessments are based on posture, grooming, attire, handshakes, eye contact and general appearance, among others. The first impression is strong and persistent. Although seemingly based on superficial characteristics, it is often accurate, because we choose how we present ourselves to others and these choices reflect our personalities. So remember, the first impression is the impression that lasts.

HOW TO MAKE A POSITIVE FIRST IMPRESSION

Finally! It was the trip that I had waited for all of my life. I was on my honeymoon and I was at Niagra Falls. I know, I know, it may sound a little old fashioned, but it was many, many moons ago that I was on my honeymoon! The point is, however, that even after all the years have passed, I will never forget the first moment that the waitress at a nice restaurant came over to take our order.

I looked up from my menu, and what I saw turned my appetite from famished to frightful. The waitress' hair was so dirty and greasy that she couldn't have washed it in weeks. Her apron and uniform had so many stains and spots on it that I could tell you what everyone had ordered that week. As she removed the pencil from her ear, she said, "Yeah...watcha' want?"

The only thing I could think was, if this is what she looks like, what does the kitchen look like? I knew I wouldn't be ordering anything.

Although this happened so many years ago I will never forget my first impression of that restaurant. Your first impression will always be the lasting impression. What image do you project?

Within the first few seconds, many impressions are formed by all of us consciously and subconsciously. Like it or not, we do judge a book by its cover. So let's dissect what our minds are programmed to look for when first meeting someone.

ONE: Handshake and Eye Contact

If you are in a service industry that greets your clients with a HANDSHAKE, that, along with the EYE CONTACT during the handshake, undoubtedly will be the very first impression. Men and women must use a firm, web to web, palm to palm, handshake with just a few gentle pumps and maintain eye contact during the entire handshake. My father used to judge my dates by their eye contact and handshake. If they had a perfect handshake and kept eye contact when they spoke with him, my curfew was midnight. However, if they had a weak handshake and little eye contact, my curfew was ten o'clock. He used to say that he couldn't trust a man who couldn't look him in the eye. I believe a feeble handshake indicates weakness or low self-esteem. I want to do business with people who are confident in themselves and the product or service they offer.

TWO: Grooming

We don't have to be beautiful, but we have to be well groomed. A local heating and air-conditioning company is one of the most impressive companies that I have ever seen. You recognize their little red trucks everywhere and they are always clean. When their service men arrive, they are clean, well groomed, tool boxes in hand are clean, and before they come in they slip surgical slippers over their shoes. They put out a towel to lay their tool box on. They never smell of cigarette smoke or sweat. They are the jewel in their industry and I believe from the care in their grooming and appearance that they are well-trained technicians.

What do you notice first when you meet a service representative? Isn't it true that you will notice their *overall* appearance? But, let's break that down to more specific items.

- First, if their hair is clean, subconsciously, your mind will put a "✓" by the O.K. hair column. However, if the hair is dirty or hanging down in someone's face, they will immediately make a negative impression.

- Second, if the customer service representative is a male and their face is not clean shaven or if they have a moustache, beard or goatee, that is not well trimmed, your mind will put a "✓" by the negative facial column.

- If the representative is a female, your subconscious mind will notice the face makeup and overall cleanliness of the face. Think about the profession that you are representing and what is the appropriate look. There are many ways to get professional suggestions on the proper way to apply make-up. Most department stores offer free make overs. (Just wear half of what they suggest when you leave!) There are many wonderfully trained consultants with major makeup companies that can give you advice as well. The bottom line is; find out what looks best on you that will help you generate a professional image. If you wear no makeup, then just make sure your face is clean.

While we are on the face, let's talk about glasses. A professional speaker friend who is very successful in the business boasts of owning 87 pairs of glasses...most being very capacious. He has done this on purpose to make himself "memorable" in a very competitive field and it works very well for him. Whatever your choice is for frames, and the look desired is up to you, just make sure that whatever you choose is applicable to your profession and most important, make sure they are cleaned often. When I am speaking to someone who has smudges and flakes on their glasses, I can't get past the film to the eyes. The eyes generally tell the story of what is at the core of most people and establishes trust and sincerity.

Your nails should be clean and trim. Of course, if you are a mechanic, we don't expect that your nails will be clean while you are working. If you are not in an industry that attracts dirt and oil, then clean them up. Better yet, treat yourself to a manicure. It can be money well invested in taking a moment to pamper yourself.

Please folks, limit your perfume! A lot of people have severe allergies and heavy perfume can really make them sick. Remember to use a "hint" not a "hit".

THREE: Attire

There is more confusion today over the definition of "business casual" than which hotel to stay in at Las Vegas! I was doing some consulting work for a major corporation and when I walked in, I was greeted by a young lady in a tank top with her bra straps showing and Capri pants so tight I could read the label of her thong underwear! What message did that send to me? What message would it send to you? It's imperative that your company define what is acceptable business casual attire. If they have no written policies, then here is a basic guideline:

Attire/Men

Shirts: Collared sport/polo shirt or button down shirt. Wear a tee shirt under shirts, but the tee shirt should not show. It's like looking at a woman's bra straps. It is never appropriate to see underwear.

Pants: Nice and clean slacks are fine. Dockers are always a nice casual pant. Jeans are not business casual; they are CASUAL. All slacks should be ironed with a crease.

Shoes: Some people notice shoes before anything else, so above all else, make sure they are clean, polished and in good repair. Loafers are best. No athletic shoes, please.

Attire/Ladies

Blouses: No see-through blouses. If we can see your bra, then you shouldn't be wearing it to work. Select nice cotton or silk blouses. I always go for easy care clothes.

Skirts: You may have beautiful legs, but in the office, mini skirts are not appropriate. No skirt should ever be shorter than holding your arm down at your side, with your hand open and the tip of your middle finger. Watch slits that are too high and if you wear a slip under your skirt (I hope you do) make sure the slip does not show at the slit.

Slacks: Same as for men, no blue jeans! Tight pants are not acceptable in the workplace...ever! They should be nicely tailored and fall about one-half inch below the top of your shoe.

Shoes: This is more of a problem for women that men. Why is it that the most "in-style" shoes always hurt the most when we wear them? Open-toed shoes are not acceptable. I do a lot of training for companies throughout the country and that is one of the factors that almost all managers ask me to address. It can be in their dress code, but women insist on breaking the rules. Toes, as a rule, aren't pretty. Cover them at work. Make sure your shoes are clean, polished, and in good repair. When they are worn out, go shopping for another comfortable shoe! (Am I really saying that to women?? Don't we all like to shop for tons of shoes??)

Remember to dress for whom you WANT to be. If you want to be perceived as promotable and professional, good grooming and dressing will never go out of style.

FOUR: Acknowledge The Customer & Be Friendly

People don't mind waiting in long lines if you are friendly and acknowledge their presence. A simple, "I'll be with you in a moment" is all that is necessary. When it is a customer's turn, acknowledge them with more than screaming "NEXT"! I hate that new word, "MAHEPU?" I can't find it in any dictionary. I am sure it *means* "May I help You?". I can't believe they mean it when they can't even say it.

If you have the opportunity to acknowledge your customer by name, use it. However, use the formal rather than the informal. Call your customer, "Mr. Jones; Ms. Smith; ma'am, or sir." When I first moved to Texas, I was amazed at being called ma'am and thought, "I'm not THAT old! Why are they calling me ma'am?" I learned that it was a respectful term used primarily in the south and I like the respect. I don't mind being called ma'am at all now. But I do not like being called "Jana" by clerks that don't know me personally. The rule is simple: use the formal name until you are invited to use the informal name.

FIVE: Be Helpful & Empathetic

It is imperative in all facets of service that you serve your customers with compassion, understanding, being responsive and sensitive to their needs. When you are dealing with an angry customer, it is sometimes hard to be empathetic. Put yourself in your customer's shoes. Why are they upset? What happened? Can you help them directly or can you find the person in your organization that can?

There is a local grocery store close to my house and the first time I walked in there, I was greeted by at least three clerks with a "Hi! How are you today?" The most amazing thing was, they waited to hear my answer. Being from California, I wondered, "What do they want?" After a few more visits, I realized that this greeting was part of their excellent training in customer service.

I came to really love shopping at Brookshires because I knew they were always empathetic to my needs and friendly in the process. Shortly after I had a leg operation, I went to Brookshires with a cast on my leg and crutches. When the manager greeted me at the door, he immediately asked what had happened. I told him it was just a little ankle operation. He then asked me if the paper I was holding in my hand was my shopping list. I told him yes. He took it from me, found me a seat in the bakery, got me a coke and cookies (yumm!) and proceeded to get my groceries! It never mattered to me from then on whether another store gave triple coupons, had better sales or more variety. My grocery dollars were spent at Brookshires.

You see, Brookshires recognized the LIFETIME VALUE of a customer. Statistics show that the average family spends $6,000.00 per year on groceries and lives an average of ten years in the area of one grocery store. Using those figures, the value of the High family was $60,000.00. That is how they treated me and I know that I have spent well over $60,000.00 in the last ten years that I have lived near Brookshires.

SIX: Be Responsive

A customer will notice immediately if you are RESPONSIVE to their needs. This breaks down simply to communication and your listening skills. Listen to your customer. You may know the answer to the customer's questions because you answer the same questions 200 times a day. However, it is the first time that customer asked you the question. Sometimes when I ask a question, a customer service representative will answer with a tone of "you should have known this, (Stupid!)."

Don't rush your customer. Do not use quick, short answers, such as Okay, Sure, Yes, Yeah, Uh-huh, and No. Respond in complete sentences. "That will be fine." "No, I am afraid we don't carry that product. I believe that [store across the street] does." You become the hero of helping the customer by responding to their needs. They may have to go elsewhere this time, but they'll be back!

SEVEN: Watch Your Attitude

What can be more important than your ATTITUDE? It shows the minute you meet your customer. It shows in so many ways: your smile, your posture, and tone of voice. You may have many other things going on in your life, but when your customer is standing in front of you, he is the only person that counts. Never make the mistake that it is someone else paying your wages. Your company only handles the money and writes the check, but it is the customer who pays your wages. Without the customer, there is no business.

A FINAL THOUGHT

It is important to remember to be courteous, confident, credible, and professional. Organizations all over the world are coming to the realization that satisfactory service is no longer acceptable. It is not a matter of keeping up or getting ahead. Exceptional customer service is a matter of survival. Your customers vote with their feet and they can walk out of your facility to your competitor in a heart beat. Remember that People are at the HEART of what we do, and service is the HEART BEAT.

You are the difference. You are the added value. Always make sure you are a valuable customer service representative and that the first impression you make is the impression that you want to last.

CHAPTER SEVEN

It's All In A Day's Work

How to be the SUPER HERO during a Customer Service Crisis

Michael Hoffman

Michael Hoffman, founder of M. Hoffman Enterprises, Inc., is an international speaker and presenter who brings with him a decade of satisfied customers and clients. The focus of his various programs is based on the following premise: "Igniting performance is about igniting people!"

Michael is a master at providing the right motivation because he has high energy and enthusiasm along with a very strong entertainment value. His great sense of humor, bolstered with his quick-wit, allows him to immediately and effectively connect and relate to his audience.

Michael does many repeat performances for companies and organizations because his audience responds so well to the messenger and ultimately the message. His message consists of programs dealing with: customer loyalty and retention, sales training and motivation, and performance management.

Effective communication combines the right informational tools with the right motivation. Motivation alone is fleeting, but the best informational tools without motivation are lifeless. He provides both.

Michael Hoffman
Carrollton, TX • 972-389-1800 • www.ignitingperformance.com

Michael Hoffman

It's All In A Days Work

How to be the SUPERHERO during a Customer Service Crisis

Mild-mannered reporter Clark Kent leaves the Daily Planet building after a hard day's work. On the roof of the building, Lois Lane, action reporter, takes off in the company helicopter on her way to a late breaking news story. Suddenly, one of the helicopter's landing railings catches under a cable, the helicopter spins out of control, crashes back to the roof, and hangs perilously over the edge. Instinctively, Lois shrieks for help as she unclasps her seat belt and attempts to scramble out the opposite door to safety. But when she flings the door open, the movement jars the helicopter, and Lois slips. As she tumbles out into the air, she grasps her seat belt buckle and is left dangling 100 stories above ground.

Clark, acutely aware that a crowd is gathering on the streets outside the Daily Planet, looks up to see the drama unfolding above him. Slipping down a back street, he enters a revolving door and, at blinding speed, emerges transformed to "Superman, The Man of Steel".

Meanwhile, Lois loses her tenuous grip on the belt buckle and with a horrified scream, plummets towards certain death. Superman, soaring to meet the damsel in distress, swoops under and gently catches her, bringing her to a stop in midair. "Steady Miss, I've got you," he soothes. Stunned, Lois clings to his neck and exclaims, "You've got me? Who's got you?!" Smiling rakishly, Superman whisks her upward toward the safety of the roof.

But before Lois can relax in Superman's solid arms, a bellow erupts from the crowd below. The helicopter has broken free from the cable and is now hurtling down towards them!

With superhero swiftness, Superman reassesses the situation. In the nick of time, he seizes the railing of the helicopter and carries Lois and the helicopter to a secure landing on the roof. Awestruck, Lois gazes up at the amazing being before her and squeaks a simple, "Thank you." In response, Superman simply smiles that smile that says, "It's all in a days work," turns toward the heavens, and flies off to the next crisis requiring his attention.

SUPERHEROES OF CUSTOMER SERVICE

Wow! How many times have you had a day like this as a customer service representative? A customer "screams" for help, you fly to the rescue, and just when you think you've averted the crisis, you see the falling helicopter. Superman expects to face problems of life and death proportions every day. It's part of his job description as a superhero. And so it is for the superheroes of customer service. You expect to face problems of "life and death" proportions every day—problems that, if not handled properly, can be death to your company's relationship with a customer. It's part of your job description. Or, as Superman says, "It's all in a day's work."

There's a quote by sales trainer extraordinaire Tom Hopkins that I live by. It says, "It's not the problem that's the problem, it's how you handle the problem that's the problem." How do you handle the problems you face daily as a customer service representative? As a superhero of customer service, do you use the superpowers that are available to you every day? Or, up until now, have you operated as a mere mortal, assuming that to possess customer service super-skills you had to be born with them?

How many of you have been to the birthing of a child? Technically all of us, yes, but I mean where you witnessed the actual birth? How many times has the doctor turned to the parents and said, "Congratulations, you have an effective customer service person"? Never, because good customer service skills are developed, not inborn. The way I like to put it is that good customer service is a skill set, not a trait. You can develop the customer service skills that will transform you from mild-mannered Clark Kent into Super Customer Serviceman in every customer service crisis you face.

THE THREE CUSTOMER SERVICE SUPER POWERS

In this chapter, we're going to focus on the three superpowers of customer service, if you will. We're going to look at how, like Superman, you can be bullet proof, utilize super hearing, and have x-ray vision in a customer service emergency.

Bullet Proof In A Customer Service Emergency

Superman can fly. He can leap tall buildings. He can see through walls. He can hear micro-sounds at macro-distances. He has the strength of, well, a superhero. But how effective would all his superpowers be if superman were vulnerable himself? If the enemy could take him out with a bullet or a flame ball or a laser ray? And how effective can you be as a customer service representative if a frustrated customer can take you down with fiery darts of rage?

Like superman, you have to be bullet proof. When you're bullet proof, you're taken out of harms way. You are separated from the emotion of the situation and you can drive more effectively toward a solution. You become impregnable to personal attacks. To be bullet proof is to take on an attitude of separating your ego from the situation, because you realize that the angry assault is not about you. The customer is furious at the company or the situation, and you represent those things to him. To be bullet proof, stems from the approach that "I am the solution; he just doesn't know it yet." You are there to serve, and the first step is the ventilation of the customer's emotions and you not taking it personally. In fact, the faster your client gets the emotions out, the faster you can move on to a solution.

The next time a customer attacks, duck into the nearest phone booth and don your suit of steel, your attitude of disassociation. Then you can tell the customer, "Go ahead and be angry. Yell it out. Scream it out. I'm not going to let it hurt me. I'm bullet proof, baby! Bring it on!" My brother-in-law is a fire fighter and paramedic. To meet him, you'd think the man couldn't have a serious bone in his body. He's got a crazy, off-the-wall personality, and he seems to live on the emotion of the moment. But when an emergency strikes, John becomes a true superhero. He throws on his emotional armor and becomes a Man of Steel. Though there is chaos around him, he's not affected by the turmoil. Nothing can penetrate his steely exterior; he is able to remain in solution mode.

It's important to realize that when you don your steely armor, you become indifferent to the turmoil, but you do not become indifferent to the person in turmoil. What kind of an emergency technician would my brother-in-law be if he were indifferent to the needs of the individual he was supposed to be helping? When you put on your superman persona, you become a person who cares for others. When you care for others, you give them a lot of slack. You allow them their emotions, their frantic ravings, their illogic. You are there to care for and protect your customers no matter what they say or how they act. You are for them, not against them. The minute you take things personally, you are no longer for them.

Once you're bullet proof and able to focus on the needs of the customer without concern for yourself, you can tap into another superpower to aid you in your attempt to rescue your client and your company from the urgent situation.

Super Hearing Customer Service Superhero

What is super hearing? Super hearing is a way of listening, of not just hearing words but understanding the emotions behind the words. An outraged customer needs to be heard, not just to communicate the reason for his frustration, but to be able to get his emotions back under control. Until that happens, the client is not able to think about the situation rationally or hear any possible solutions.

In a crisis, logic goes away when emotions go up. As a customer service superhero, it is imperative that you find a way to help the client bring his emotions and logic back into balance so you can move toward a solution. First, allow the customer to vent. Hear between the words and label the feelings. Say the feelings back to the customer. It's called showing empathy. Show your client he's being heard. I show them that I'm listening not only to their problem, but also to them as a person by labeling their feelings. Being heard, for most people, is the same as being loved. It's the act of being heard that balances the emotion.

As the client becomes aware that he has an audience receptive to his grievances, he will begin to cool down. When that happens, logic will begin to have equal footing with emotion, and you and the customer will be able to more effectively look at options for solving the dilemma.

The customer of a national insurance company was fuming. He had received a bill for his monthly premium, and the company had overcharged him—again! He thought he had taken care of the problem the month before. As he dialed the customer service number listed on his bill, he continued to stew about the financial gouging he had taken from the insurance industry, and about the fact that he was often treated as little more than a number in a machine.

When the unsuspecting customer service representative answered the phone with a cheery, "Thank you for calling...," she was immediately hit with a deluge of heated words, including some specific references to her ineptitude. The representative actively listened with responses like, "yes," "I see," and "tell me more." She used super hearing to diffuse his wrath by attempting to label his feelings with comments like "Really, that is frustrating," "I can see why you'd be upset," and "I'd be angry too if I thought the problem was fixed and it showed up on my bill again."

Almost immediately, the customer began to lose the venom in his voice and to express legitimate issues like, "I'm angry because I don't have any confidence that this will be handled right. The customer service superhero was then able to address the customer's predicament with some potential solutions.

It's not always easy to listen to an angry person. Sometimes it takes a lot of listening and responding to balance the emotional position the customer is in. Don't rush the process.

I have a friend, Amy, who used to be a negotiator for a company that handled contracts with a group of teamsters. Now Amy is just a waif of a woman, and once they sent in their biggest, toughest negotiator to haggle with her. For 8 hours this teamster tried to gain a mental advantage by belittling and verbally harassing Amy into submission. Ah, but Amy was smart. She used super hearing to maintain her edge. Every time he attacked her with heightened emotion, she remained calm and responded with empathy. At the end of a very productive day her counterpart said to her, "You know, it's hard to be an S.O.B. if you're not going to be one too."

When using super hearing, don't be afraid to mislabel the feelings of the customer. If you do miss the mark, your customer will probably correct you, but the impact of being heard on a personal level will still have its affect. The heightened emotional state of the customer will start to balance out.

Once super hearing allows you to bring the crisis situation to a place where logic can be applied to find a solution, it's time to bring the third superpower into operation. It's time to use your x-ray vision.

SuperHero Customer Service Representative with X-Ray Vision

X-ray vision helps you to "see" a solution that would not be obvious to you without it. It brings you into the realm of creativity. The words "there is no solution" do not exist for a superhero when he is able to apply x-ray vision.

The customer doesn't share your x-ray vision. He has no idea what options are available for handling the situation, what resources he can tap into or how your company works. When emotions ruled his thinking, the customer had only one answer to his problem...your heart on a platter. But once logic returns, he is often at a loss to come up with a viable solution. That's your job. Now is the time for your x-ray vision to see the myriad of options available to you so you can go beyond your client's expectations and present them to him.

A technician at a duplicating service I use here in Dallas is a marvelous example of someone with x-ray vision. Once her company duplicated and delivered over five hundred copies of one of my seminar videos to be used at a conference I was holding two days later. Unfortunately, the picture and sound quality of the videos I received was terrible. There was no way I could accept the shipment, but without it I would not have the product I needed at my conference.

I immediately called the duplicating service and told the receptionist of my predicament, knowing there was little or no chance that anything could be done about it. To my surprise she put me through to a technician who suggested I bring the originals in right away. After viewing them, the technician was confident that she could adjust the color and sound to get a better master to work with.

But that would only solve part of my problem. How was I going to get five hundred copies made, stuffed, and delivered in time for my conference.

The technician had a brainstorm. She got permission to have an all night emergency packing party. With the help of her co-workers and some of my friends, we duplicated, quality checked, stuffed, and readied for shipping all five hundred copies of my product that night. The technician personally made sure the tapes were shipped to my conference site. It was her x-ray vision that helped her look past the obvious to an extraordinary solution Needless to say, I consider her company, not just a vendor, but a true partner in my business.

See Past The Obvious To Create A Solution

Perhaps, like the customer you're trying to help, you don't believe there are many options either. You think your hands are tied; that there's not much you can do to remedy the situation. There is always a solution. You have to determine right now that you will always try to see past the obvious to a creative answer beyond expectations.

Maybe you think you don't have the power or authority to put forth an alternative solution. Suppose you have an irate customer who insists that there is nothing that will make him happy (short of your heart on a platter). You know that if you can find a way to make this customer happy, even though your company may take a hit on this particular transaction, you could end up with a satisfied customer loyal to your company for many sales in the future. You go to your manager and negotiate. "Here's the deal. This guy is beyond furious. Nothing I've suggested as a solution is making him feel better about the situation. Suppose we give him a ridiculous discount, cut our losses and simply comp him the merchandise. We take a loss this time, but when he hangs up the phone, he feels good about our company. Instead of making the sale while losing the client, we lose the sale but keep the client, maybe for a long time to come."

What do you think your manager would say to such a proposal? Was it creative enough? Maybe he'd think you were out to lunch. You'll never know unless you give it a shot, unless you learn to think outside the box, to use your x-ray vision to see past the obvious.

Have you heard the story of the young man working behind the counter at a national parcel delivery service? A customer came to him with an item for delivery and demanded, "This package absolutely has to arrive by tomorrow morning." Even though it was past the cut-off time for guaranteed delivery, the youth promised, "No problem. We will deliver the package on time. You have our guarantee." However, the package missed the bus that was to take it to the airport.

What would you have done in that situation? It was just a little package, worth about $12, but worth infinitely more to the customer. Can you "see" any solutions to the problem? Well, this young man definitely had x-ray vision. He saw past the obvious to a creative solution. He hired a helicopter to pick up the package and deliver it to Kennedy airport! The customer's package made its flight out and was delivered on time as promised.

Customer Service Creativity

What would your manager say to such a drastic way of handling the problem? The next day, a top level executive of this national parcel delivery company received an enthusiastic phone call from the customer, praising his company for getting his package to its destination on time as he had been promised.

That same day the executive made a special visit to the little branch office and approached the manager, and inquired about the outrageous expense. After hearing the entire story, the executive insisted that the young man receive commendations for going beyond expectations and thinking creatively in his job as a customer service representative. He also suggested the man be instructed as to his spending boundaries and be told what personnel resources to tap into if he should ever find himself in such a situation again.

Most of us get hung up on the idea that the higher ups in the company would never approve of our unusual ideas if there is no profit in them. But, in reality, most managers will always say yes to your attempt to satisfy your customers beyond their expectations.

So, there you have them, three of the superpowers of customer service. Use them the next time you are facing a customer service crisis. And when, in the end, you are able to save the day, I want you to stand up from your desk, put your shoulders back, and fill your chest with pride. And, as your hands sweep across your hips, shout with bravado for all to hear, "I am CUSTOMER SERVICE MAN!"

It's not that we need to be more like superheroes. It's that we are superheroes. Doing it everyday, on purpose, as a skill set. It's just ALL IN A DAY'S WORK.

CHAPTER EIGHT

The Service Advantage

How to Create a Competitive Edge and Improve Customer Retention

JP Maroney

"The business executive's worst fear is that their people won't care as much as they do about the organization's success," says JP Maroney. As a business strategist, author and professional speaker, JP helps organizations leverage their human capital by creating entrepreneurial corporate cultures where people at every level think and act like owners. "Most employees will never go out and start their own company, but given the opportunity, tools, and motivation they will treat the organization as if it is their own," says Maroney.

JP Maroney's strategies include:

- How to lead a mission-guided organization
- How to get people to "buy-in" to your vision
- How to improve employee morale and reduce turnover
- How to foster creativity and innovation within people
- 5 master keys to building great teams
- How to remove barriers to speed and agility
- How to implement change without killing morale
- How to create a customer-focused corporate culture
- How to foster an entrepreneurial spirit in people

JP Maroney International
Tyler, TX • 800-304-5758 • www.JPMaroney.com

JP Maroney

The Service Advantage

How to Create a Competitive Edge and Improve Customer Retention

When it comes to competing in today's marketplace, there's bad news and good news. The bad news is that this year alone, poor service will cost the average American company up to thirty percent of its customers.

The good news is that companies that implement effective customer retention programs can expect to see profits rise by twenty to one hundred percent. Why? Because it's more cost effective to keep customers.

A study by the Forum Corporation revealed that it costs roughly one-fifth the amount of money to service an existing customer as it does to attract a new customer. That means that replacing a customer is five times more costly than retaining existing customers.

Superior customer service pays. In fact, not only can it be a powerful tool for retaining customers; it can also be an important factor in attracting new customers. Great service can create a buzz about your organization in the marketplace. That word of mouth can be one of your company's most effective and efficient marketing tools.

I'm about to give you information that will help your organization create a competitive advantage by offering superior customer service.

This chapter includes four segments.

1. In the first segment, you'll learn how to identify your real customers.
2. In segment two you'll learn a three-step formula for discovering what your customers really expect.
3. In segment three you'll learn how to deliver value to every customer, every time.
4. And, finally, in segment four you'll learn how you and your organization can gain a competitive edge by offering superior customer service.

1. SO, WHO ARE YOUR CUSTOMERS?

The quick answer is...the people who buy your company's products or services. Right? But, that's not the only type of customer. There are actually two different types of customers, external and internal.

External Customers

External customers are typically the end user who actually pays for your product or service. On the other hand, if your organization is a manufacturer, or franchiser, your external customers may include independent distributors, retailers, or franchisees.

External customers are fairly easy to identify. In fact, most employees, when asked to identify their customer, give an example of an external customer.

The external customer is, in fact, a very important customer, one to be valued. But individuals and organizations make a big mistake when they focus strictly on serving external customers to the exclusion of internal customers.

Internal Customers

Internal customers include other individuals or departments within your organization that depend on you or your department. It could include co-workers, and even your boss.

Providing effective service to internal customers is just as important, in fact, sometimes more important than serving external customers. Here's why.

When we fail to provide quality service to our internal customers, our external customers usually suffer as well. There's a very vital link between serving internal and external customers. Each depends on the other.

So, how do you effectively serve your internal customers? First, there must be a paradigm shift in who you believe to be your real customers. Many employees don't even think they have customers since they never deal with external customers. That's a mistake.

Every person in your organization has at least one customer. Most people have more than one. It might be that you have both internal and external customers. In an organization that is using customer service to create a competitive advantage, every person, at every level, must be focused on service customers effectively. That includes internal and external customers.

Once you make that paradigm shift, and realize that no matter what your job title, you do have customers, you're ready to provide effective customer service. Here's one way to look at it.

Begin to think of yourself as an independent business owner. That's right. You incorporated. And then begin to think of the other people in your organization who depend on you as your customers. Now, begin treating those customers with the same level of service you expect when you are the customer.

Additionally, if you're a member of a team or department, your group can begin to think of itself as an independent company. You guessed it...Accounting Incorporated. It's much easier to think of those who are dependent on us as customers when we view ourselves as being an important business unit...a valuable part of the organization.

The next step is to identify what your customers expect. That is the focus of our next section.

2. IDENTIFYING CUSTOMER EXPECTATIONS

Have you heard the phrase, "don't offer a solution until you know the problem?" When it comes to using quality service to exceed customer expectations, I say, "don't try to exceed customer expectations until you know what they expect." Make sense?

It's really not that hard to discover precisely what your customers want. Let me give you a three-part formula for identifying your customer's expectations.

Number one, think like a customer. Number two, ask the customer. And, number three, listen to the customer.

Think Like A Customer

Thinking like a customer is easy. We're all customers, right? After all, every day we spend our hard-earned money buying products and services from other companies. So, it should be pretty easy to think like a customer.

And that's what I challenge you to do. Take a few minutes to answer the question: "If I were a customer of your organization, what would I expect?"

Ask the Customer

Obviously, if you want a complete picture of what a customer expects, you need to go directly to the source and ASK the customer what they expect.

Questions are one of the most powerful tools you have in communication. And they can be one of your most powerful tools in discovering what your customers really expect. Remember that customers can be both internal and external.

- Is there any special service you would like us to provide?
- What can we do to improve the way we serve you?
- What do you expect when you do business with us?
- How satisfied are you with the level of service we currently provide?

You might even get more specific, for example, and ask…

- Are you pleased with how fast you get through the check-out line?
- Are the hours that we are open sufficient for you to conveniently do business with our organization?
- Do you feel welcome when you come into our company?
- Are you satisfied with our delivery times?

No doubt about it, we MUST ask questions if we really want to know what customers expect. I believe that many times we don't ask the questions because we are afraid of the answers. Perhaps we're afraid the customer will demand something we are incapable of providing. But, that's usually not the case. And the benefits of using questions to discover what customers really want make them well worth the risk.

Listen to Customers

Finally, listening to customers can also be an excellent tool for discovering what they expect. You've most likely had customers share improvements they would like to see. Sometimes they don't tell us directly. Instead, we overhear them talking to another customer or one of our co-workers.

Either way, listening is a powerful tool. The key is to take time to truly listen to what the other person is saying. I often say that most of us are not really listening. Instead, we're just waiting to speak. We're thinking to ourselves, "If they'll just shut up I'll say what I've got to say."

When it comes to serving customers, listening can provide you with important insight into what the customer really expects. I'll bet that within the last week or two, you've heard at least one of your internal customers express their feelings about improvements they would like to see.

Customer expectations will be different for every company, but one expectation common with every customer is VALUE.

3. PROVIDING HIGH VALUE

I've asked a number of people in my live seminars to define value. Most of the time they have difficulty doing so. We all have a sense of what value is, but have a hard time putting it into words.

Let me give you a definition you can remember. When the benefit received is greater than the price paid, value is perceived. Now, notice I said that value is perceived. That's because value is intangible. It is a perception in the customer's mind.

That's why one customer can come into your place of business and say, "Wow, your prices are great." And, the very next customer can come in and say, "Good grief, your prices are high." Again, value is perceived.

It's the responsibility of you and every person in your organization to work at increasing the level of perceived value in the mind of each customer. You can do that by learning how to communicate the benefits of doing business with your organization.

So, what are the benefits of doing business with your organization? Before we answer that question, I want to make an important distinction between benefits and features.

Features are the attributes of your product or service. For example, if you were talking about an automobile, the features might include air bags, fuel efficiency, or sturdy construction. If you were talking about a company's features, you might include covered parking, extended hours of operation, or twenty-five years in business.

Defining the features of your product or service is the first step in defining the benefits to the customer.

Yet, while features are an important part of the equation, they don't communicate value to the customer. You must translate those features into benefits. The benefit is what the product or service actually does for the customer.

In the example of the automobile, the air bag feature could be translated into benefits like saving lives, and reducing the likelihood of serious injury in an accident. In the example of the company's features, the extended hours of operation could be translated into a benefit of convenience to the consumer.

Customers Don't Buy Features, They Buy Benefits If we want to communicate the benefits of buying our products or service, we must translate every feature into customer benefits. An easy way to do this is to look at each feature and answer the questions, "What's in it for the customer?"

4. THE SLIGHT EDGE

No one can argue with the fact that we are in a service-driven economy. Customers today are expecting more than they have ever expected, and many want to pay less for it.

Now, simply satisfying customers is not enough to keep them from defecting to the competition. Instead, what is required is a company-wide focus on doing extra things, beyond what customers expect, which will differentiate the company from it's competitors.

I call this the slight edge! In any competition, including business, the little things can make a big difference. Sometime back I was watching three Olympic hopefuls who happened to be sisters running in the same qualifying race. Coming down the final stretch, two of the sisters were in first and second place while the third sister was in fourth place, At the finish line, the third sister leaned forward at the very last moment and captured third place. And with that, the three sisters were all headed for the Olympics.

We've seen the same scenario in horse races, auto races, and triathlons. Many times, there's just a slight difference between the winner and everyone else.

Business is no different. Companies can gain a competitive advantage by focusing on the little things.

One of our clients is an air conditioning contractor that was looking for little things that would differentiate them from competitors. One of their service technicians suggested that they check and change the batteries in customer's smoke detectors when they made their semi-annual service visits.

Now, that's a little thing, but it makes a big difference. The company president told me that one of their customers personally thanked him for the value-added service. It turns out the service technician had discovered a smoke detector in one of the customer's rental properties that didn't even have a battery in it.

A few months ago, I drove through at a hamburger establishment with my wife, daughter, and two little dogs. When the employee at the window gave us our food, she also passed us two doggy biscuits for our dogs. A little thing? Yes! A big difference? You bet!

Our bank has the same practice of passing out doggy biscuits. And we remember that.

I shared that story at a seminar sometime back, and one of the participants said, "Yeah, my bank used to give out doggy biscuits too, then they stopped, and my dogs have come to expect it." So, be careful that you continue doing the little things that customers enjoy.

A fire chief recently shared with me that his organization gives out a special packet of information and supplies to victims who's home has burned. It's an appreciated service at a very inconvenient time. Again, it's a little thing.

The fact is, little things don't have to be difficult, and they don't have to be expensive. I challenge you to look for little things that will give your organization a competitive advantage. Use your imagination and be creative.

These little things will make you and your organization more memorable. Most of all, they will make your organization more competitive.

Your Competitive Advantage

No doubt about it, customer service can be a powerful factor in giving your organization a competitive advantage. Today's customer demands the highest level of service. And if they don't get it from you, they'll go someplace else.

Let's review what we covered in this chapter.

- First, there are two types of customers, internal and external.
- Second, there are three keys for identifying what your customers expect. Think like a customer, ask the customer, and listen to the customers.
- Third, every customer expects value. You can raise the level of perceived value in the mind of your customers by communicating the benefits provided by your product or service.
- And finally, to be truly competitive in today's marketplace you need the slight edge. And, you can gain that slight edge using the little things to differentiate your organization from the competition.

CHAPTER NINE

Peanut Butter and Pickles

The Art Of Effective Customer Service Communication

Bernadette Trujillo-Vadurro

Dynamic, energetic, enthusiastic and highly motivational are words audiences across the country use to describe Bernadette Trujillo-Vadurro. Bernadette produces customized training programs using multi-media technology, accelerated learning techniques and industry specific content.

Bernadette is a Magna Cum Laude graduate from the College of Santa Fe with a degree in Business Management. The Rio Grande Minority Purchasing Council selected Bernadette as the Minority Women Supplier in 1999. She has been listed in Who's Who Worldwide and Oxford's Who's Who in Business and is the president of Leading Edge Training Technologies.

Mrs. Trujillo-Vadurro has trained many distinguished organizations including the Chrysler Corporation, American Express, Los Alamos National Laboratory, Columbia Hospital Corporation, Indian Health Services, Pittsburgh Housing Authority and the Central Intelligence Agency. Her topics include World Class Customer Service, Thinking Outside The Box, Change Management, Public Speaking Skills, Motivation and Attitude Improvement, Stress Management, Communication Skills, Diversity and Leadership Training.

Leading Edge Training Technologies
Santa Fe, NM • 800-736-8986 • www.letraining.com

Bernadette Trujillo-Vadurro

Peanut Butter and Pickles

The Art Of Effective Customer Communication

Have you ever made a bunch of peanut butter sandwiches? You always have to wash your hands afterwards because you get the sticky stuff all over you. How about when you eat a pickle? Eating a pickle is similar to eating a clove of garlic; you can smell pickle on your breath for hours afterward. Peanut butter and pickles represent the perceptions that stick in our customers' minds when they do business with us. This chapter offers a practical guide to better customer service using these analogies. In the next few pages we will be discussing listening skills, recognizing customer types, avoiding customer service deadly sins and forbidden phrases. We will examine how to employ user-friendly responses and the importance of body language in customer service communication.

PEANUT BUTTER RULE 1

Be Cognizant of How You Listen - Making Sandwiches and Running Marathons

We live in a society that applauds multi-tasking: the ability to do several things simultaneously. Unfortunately, one can rarely listen effectively while engaged in other activities. Perhaps you have experienced a situation in which you have been talking with a service person while they were multi-tasking, i.e., entering data on a computer, talking to another person, writing something down or having a telephone conversation with a third party on the telephone. What does that service person's face look like when they are multi-tasking and listening to you at the same time? Do you notice the blank face, glazed eyes, and detached head nodding? The blank face and glazed eyes are usually accompanied by a series of "a-ha's" or "I sees" directed your way. Despite the verbal reassurances, you are quite sure this person hasn't understood a word you have said. According to psychologist, Susan Baile, Ph.D., there are four basic modes of listening:[1] pretend, autobiographical, empathetic and reflective. The first mode of listening called pretend listening is the type of listening described above and isn't really listening at all.

The second mode of listening is called autobiographical listening. This type of listening, according to Dr. Baile, is listening to tell your story or listening to hear yourself speak.

I like to think of effective listening and communicating as a tennis or volleyball game. As long as the ball continues moving back and forth between the players, the game is in play. However, when the ball goes off the court, the play stops. When we engage in pretend listening the game never really starts and when we engage in autobiographical listening we shoot one-shot balls that immediately bounce off the court.

PEANUT BUTTER RULE # 2

Use Empathetic and Reflective Listening Skills - Add Peanut Butter to Apples or Celery

The next two types of listening have the capacity to change relationships. They are empathetic and reflective listening. When you are engaged in empathetic listening, you are listening to understand the situation or concern. You do not engage in judgment nor are you busy thinking about your response. Instead, you are interested in understanding what the communicator is sharing with you.

The highest level of listening is called reflective listening. It includes empathetic listening skills as it takes listening to a higher level. Have you ever been engaged in a conversation in which you shared information with another person and the responses were right on target- so much so that you knew your listener fully understood your message? Your listener was not only able to understand, but also able to summarize and paraphrase the content of the message back to you with full empathy and understanding. If you have experienced this phenomenon, chances are you have experienced reflective listening.

One of the primary issues in customer service communication is the fact that many of our employees have not been trained in the art of listening. Empathetic and reflective listening requires practice and concentration. Learning these skills may also mean we must break old habits such as interrupting and finishing others' sentences, being easily distracted or mentally arguing with our customers. So, how can we become better listeners? A technique I learned from communication expert, Debra Sutch[2], was to observe the eye color of the person with whom you are communicating. This deep look into their eyes causes you, the listener, to get focused on the individual with whom you are communicating. In the American business world direct eye contact says, "I'm listening and interested." I highly recommend you program the following thought projection into your mind's eye when communicating with others. The thought is "this is the most important person in the world at this moment." What do you believe the quality of your conversations will be like if you get focused, look for the person's eye color and then think "this is the most important person in the world at this moment" as you engage in empathetic and reflective listening? Most people agree this would dramatically increase the quality of all conversations.

PEANUT BUTTER RULE # 3

Recognize Your Customer Type – Smooth, Creamy or Crunchy

According to Dr. Rick Brickman, author of Dealing with People you Can't Stand: How to Bring Out the Best in People at Their Worst[3], there are several different types of customers. We need to actively listen to our customers in order to determine their type and formulate appropriate responses. The following shows customer types and their primary intention.

TYPE 1 - Get it done: This customer needs your assistance immediately! He/she wanted it yesterday.

TYPE 2 - Get it right: This customer wants to ensure the information or service is accurate.

TYPE 3 - Get acknowledged: This customer suffers from low self-esteem. He/she needs ego stroking.

TYPE 4 - Get along: This customer's motto is "live and let live." He/she just wants to get along with others.

Listening to determine customer type is essential to understanding customers and helps you to provide a matching response. Many employees are "Get it Done" types while many customers may be other "Get it" types. Recognizing this fact requires flexibility in our responses. Here's an example of a Get it Done Customer Service Representative communicating with a Get it Right Customer.

The Get it Right Customer says, "I want to make sure this information is confirmed before we schedule a second appointment."

The Get it Done Customer Service Representative responds, "We can schedule that appointment either next week or the following week. Which week would you prefer?"

The customer becomes flustered. He feels that the Customer Service Representative is not listening, because his response does not address the issue of wanting the confirmation of information prior to scheduling another appointment. In order to provide excellent customer service, the Get it Done Customer Service Representative must provide a congruent Get it Right response. An example of a Get it Right response is:

"I will be happy to verify and confirm the information prior to scheduling a second appointment for you."

Let's take another example. Imagine that you are a Get it Right Customer Service Representative dealing with a Get Acknowledged Customer. Remember, Get Acknowledged types suffer from low self-esteem. An underlying purpose in their communication is to obtain ego strokes from you. While on the other hand, as a Get it Right Customer Service Representative, you recognize the company has certain policies and procedures which you are committed to following.

The Get Acknowledged Customer states, "My family has been doing business with your company for 35 years and you're still asking for identification?"

A typical Get it Right Customer Service Representative's response is, "Sir, our company policy requires identification for this form of transaction."

A more appropriate response would include acknowledging the customer by using his or her name and saying something like:

"Mr. Jones, we appreciate your loyalty and dedication as a customer. However, we ask for identification only to ensure your protection." In both these examples, by flexing our communication to create congruent responses, we become advocates of our customers and thereby increase customer service effectiveness.

PICKLE RULE # 1

Avoid the Eight Deadly Sins – Even Breath Mints Won't Help

In my research I have determined there are at least eight deadly sins in customer service. They are as follows:

1. Ignoring the customer.
2. Over-promising and under-delivering.
3. Being passed around from one person to the next when trying to resolve a problem.
4. Tardy, delayed, wrong, inadequate or incomplete goods or services.
5. Incompetent staff.
6. Failure to take responsibility for mistakes.
7. Blaming the customer, other staff, management or the organization.
8. Giving preferential treatment without justification.

Let me expand on deadly sin # 2: Over-promising and under-delivering. This deadly sin is commonly practiced upon many American consumers causing frustration and ill feelings. Consumers are told that car repairs will take only one day and the repairs end up taking a week. Customers are promised delivery of goods within 3 to 5 working days and the delivery arrives 3 weeks later. Customers are told a project or installation will cost $1,500.00 and it ends up costing $2,300.00. Every time you over-commit by saying you will do things at certain times and at certain prices and under-deliver by failing to meet promised deadlines or charging more than agreed, you cut away at your credibility.

I encourage you to "slightly pad" wait times as well as estimated costs to customers. By engaging in this padding practice, you always provide services and goods slightly ahead of schedule and slightly below cost thereby greatly increasing your customers' perceptions.

PICKLE RULE # 2

Recognize Forbidden Phrases –Spicier Pickles Have A Longer Lasting Affect

Forbidden phrases are certain word choices that may cause our customers to feel alienated or negative towards our business and us.

1. "No" – Any customer service statement that starts with the word "No" causes immediate alienation.

2. "I don't know" – Customers are not interested in what you do not know. They are interested in what you do know.

3. "You'll have to…" This statement makes the hair stand up on the back of your customer's head. The only thing your customer has to do is breath and at some point die!

4. "Our policy states" – Your customers don't care about your policies. You must think of another way to say this. Some examples are "for your protection" or "in order to expedite."

5. "But" - Anytime you say "but", you negate the statement you previously made. Here is an example, "We appreciate your business, but we can't help you." Instead, you may want to say "We appreciate your business and let's see who will be able to help you."

6. "It's not my job" - Your customers aren't concerned with what is or isn't your job. They simply need help and you are the one with whom they are speaking. Instead, say "Let me direct you to the person who can assist you with this."

7. "I can't" – Customers are not interested in what you cannot do for them. Tell them instead what you can do for them.

8. "It's your problem" – If it is your customer's problem then it's also likely to be your problem as well. Be careful when using the word "problem". It's a red flag word that can often be perceived as negative. As an alternative, use words like, "challenge", "situation" or "issue."

PEANUT BUTTER RULE # 4

Employ User Friendly Responses – For Extra Flavor Add Jam or Honey

We get into trouble when we don't have readily available alternatives to forbidden phrases. I have designed a series of statements called "User Friendly Statements" which can be used in lieu of a forbidden phrase.

Here are a few examples:

1. Let me explain...
2. The reason...
3. How would you like to resolve this issue?
4. Let me review your request.
5. I'll be happy to find out who handles...
6. For your protection…
7. For your convenience…
8. In order to expedite…

Instead of saying Forbidden Phrase #1 "No", you can use User Friendly Response # 1 "Let me explain…" or # 2 "The reason…" Instead of using Forbidden Phrase #6 "It's not my job" you can use User Friendly Response #5 "I'll be happy to find out who handles…" Another alternative to using Forbidden Phrase #3, "You'll have to…", is to consider using User Friendly Response # 7 "For your convenience…"

PEANUT BUTTER RULE # 5

How you say it Tells All[4] – Peanut Butter is a Good Source of Protein

Dr. Albert Mehrabian of the University of California, UCLA, conducted one of the most interesting studies in communication. In his work, Dr. Mehrabian demonstrated the importance of tonality, facial expressions and body language in the delivery of a verbal message.

Visual elements are made up of body language, appearance and facial expressions. Dr. Mehrabian found that 55% of your message when speaking to another person is interpreted by the way you stand as well as the expressions you make on your face and your general appearance. In order to provide top-notch services to your customers you must pay attention to your body orientation. Are you facing customers with an interested look on your face? Is your body language saying "I'm ready to serve you?" Are you maintaining respectful eye contact and showing concern in your face and eyes when speaking and listening to your customer? Are your gestures open and positive while communicating? Remember, your body language expresses the degree of attention and willingness you mentally project to your customer. For example, if a service person says, "I'm happy to help you" but you see the service person staring blankly at you and you hear a cold or indifferent tone of voice, what you interpret is an "I could care less" attitude.

Tonality makes up 38% of the communicated message. Tonality establishes the overall quality of your voice. Is your tone of voice straightforward, honest, pleasant and easy to listen to? Do you have a moderate to deep-pitched voice and do you modulate your voice speed to make sure you sound intelligent and interesting, never speaking too slowly or too rapidly?

Since words constitute 7% of the message, words are still important. Politeness never goes out of style. Don't forget common courtesies such as "please", "thank you" and "may I" in your every day customer service interactions.

In this short chapter we have covered a lot of ground. To ensure customer service excellence in your organization remember the five peanut butter and three pickle rules: become more cognizant of your listening skills; employ empathetic and reflective listening, recognize your customer by type and respond congruently. Employ user-friendly responses as you pay attention to your body language and tonality. Avoid the eight deadly sins and learn to identify forbidden phrases. Like peanut butter and pickles, I hope you can make these concepts stick to your organizational culture to make a positive difference in your customer service interactions!

References:

1. Baile, Susan, Ph.D. "Building Self-Esteem in Your Child", Career Track, 1991.
2. Sutch, Debra, "Interpersonal Communication Skills", Career Track, 1996.
3. Brinkman, Rick and Rick, Kirschner, "Dealing With People You Can't Stand: How to Bring Out the Best in People at Their Worst", McGraw-Hill, December 1994.
4. UCLA Albert Mehrabian, Ph.D., "Silent Messages", Mehrabian & Ferris, 1967.

CHAPTER TEN

GLEE = MC^{2*}

A Formula For Awesome Customer Service

KELLI VRLA

VRLA (pron.Ver-lah) noun/verb/adj. 1. funny, entertaining, 2. informative, 3. motivating, exciting and Greek.

An enthusiastic "ENTERTRAINER," Kelli Vrla is a Road Warrior for humor in your life. A proven sales and marketing performer for over 16 years in the broadcasting industry, Kelli V has generated millions of dollars with her festive techniques.

No stranger to humor, Kelli V spent several years performing stand-up comedy, appeared on *CBS This Morning*, opened for Phyllis Diller, and was a runner up in Joan Rivers' America's Funniest Woman Contest.

In hundreds of humor workshops in North and Central America, as well as in Europe and Mexico, Kelli V teaches relevant, memorable and immediately-transferable skills to harness creative, effective ways to be less stressed and more productive.

Humor At Work International
Dallas, TX • 214-987-4242 • www.kelliv.com

Kelli Vrla

GLEE = MC^{2}*

A Formula For Awesome Customer Service

In my travels (150 on-the-road speaking days per year) I've seen both great and unbelievably poor service. In this quick recap on exceptional customer service, I'm going to note a few personal examples of great and not-so-great service I've received, then give you the formula that inspires awesome customer handling.

*(MC^{2} = More-Satisfied Customers, Too!)

NOT-SO-GREAT SERVICE ENCOUNTERS

We've all experienced horrific customer service at one time or another. My travels lend to more opportunities than most, and I am continually amazed at how companies still stay in business using these practices. I am convinced that one of our greatest disservices to customers is NOT knowing the level of service we give them (or fail to give them) on a daily basis.

HOTEL HELL

Let's start with hotel clerks who announce my ROOM NUMBER loudly to the entire lobby (always a thrill for the woman traveling alone). Somewhere, they may have been told this is a no-no, but they need to be reminded to point silently to the room number instead. They also need to be told the reason for this practice.

Then, there's my experience at a Miami South Beach Hotel

where my non-smoking room greeted me with cigarette butts overflowing in an ashtray.

My all-time favorite hotel story happened at something like a "Motel 3" (I'm guessing they couldn't afford the other 3 numbers). After many flight delays, I arrived at the hotel way past midnight. The following dialogue ensued:

Clerk: "Your room number is 243, the last room in the inn. There's no lock on the door; is that a problem?"
Me: " I think it might be."
Clerk: "Oh, it's no big deal, really. C'mon let me show you." (Huffing up 2 flights of stairs, carrying my own bags, since he did not offer to take them because, he explained, he was not a "porter," he was just a "desk clerk".) We arrived at the door, and I saw that not only was the lock missing, the entire doorknob was gone, leaving a gaping hole in the door.
Clerk: (from the hallway looking at me inside the room through the large hole in the door) "Seeeee, it's not that big a deal!"
Me: (wanting to strangle him) "Well, I guess it depends on which side of the door you're on."

It always depends on which side of the door we're on when giving or receiving customer service.

Other honorable mentions in poor service:

- A flight attendant who seemed bothered that I asked her to open the can of pop for me
- Employees engaged in conversation with each other who looked peeved that I needed to interrupt them for service
- The phone company representative who hung up on me when I had a legitimate (and calmly-stated) complaint
- Having to leave a fitting room after completely re-dressing to retrieve another size of the same item, because no salesclerks were in sight
- Having a cell phone-payment refused at a local cellular chain store because it was "not set up to take payments"

- Hearing an IT worker justify her flippancy with "stupid" customers because—in her opinion--they are "so stupid"
- The airline gate agent who refused to transfer my ticket to another airline to avoid the blizzard connection (and probable cancellation) of my scheduled flight, saying, "We don't have a reciprocal agreement with ___ Airlines." I went all the way outside--through security--and found another agent (with the same airline) who was only too happy to oblige the transfer, saying," Oh, sure, no problem----hope you make it to your seminar."

There's an overall malaise in many areas of customer service. We have to be diligent to convey the need to respect the customers who provide us our jobs. We must try to instill pride in our people so they have a vested interest in sincerely serving the customer.

THE FLIP SIDE – THE JAW-DROPPING SERVICE

I have had my share of great service, albeit it a rare commodity:

- Have Credit Card, Will Travel: Because it didn't take credit cards, a pizza chain (Cici's) treated me to its dinner buffet. When I insisted I'd make an ATM run and return with cash, the manager said, "Don't worry about it. You're welcome here; I know you'll come back." (I have returned many, many times all over the country and have told this story countless times.)
- The hotel manager who drove to my seminar to return valuable items left in the room after I had checked out.
- The waiter, who heard the clink of my fork, turned on his heel to clear my plate (knowing he was NOT my server and might NOT get a tip. This reminds me of the "boundaryless" corporation GE's Jack Welch talks about: doing what needs to be done, with no boundaries on our job descriptions.)
- The staff at the Kansas City International Airport American Airlines Admiral's Club, who drop by to see if they can freshen up my diet soda, who anticipate I'll need to work on my computer, who tell me---by the way---there's a spare room in the back where I can get some work done.

- RESTAURANT TRAINING SQUAD: While visiting between shifts, I heard the manager point out, "You're here to serve the people without them noticing you're here. They're having a wonderful, tasty lunch and somehow their water glass is refilled and they don't know how it got that way. Your job is to be invisible. Do you hear me? Invisible, but oh, so necessary!"

LOOM SERVICE: RECOGNIZING THE COMMON THREADS OF AWESOME CUSTOMER SERVICE

The preceding vignettes might have given you a glimpse of common to do's and taboos of exceptional service. In a nutshell, my extensive research has led me to see that many common threads of crafting superb service have been well-articulated by Southwest Airlines. Simple, relevant, memorable and easily transferable---Southwest weaves all the threads needed for a warm blanket of success.

I have had the esteemed privilege of training some of Southwest's finest employees, and I can say---firsthand—they live and breathe this stuff; they truly practice what they preach.

SOME SOUTHWEST AIRLINES SIMPLE SERVICE SUCCESS SECRETS:

1. DO What You Ask of Others

"One reason Southwest employees continue to provide legendary service is that they are led by leaders who know what it means to serve." (NUTS! , Kevin & Jackie Freiberg,) I personally witness this on many of my flights. On my last trip, the Captain was fully engaged in clearing trash from the plane to prepare for the next set of passengers. It is not uncommon for Herb Kelleher (President)—as well as other top company officers--to help hoist baggage during Southwest's busiest holiday periods.

2. The More Employees Know, the More they Care.

"Inform your people; it teaches them to care." (NUTS!) When you arm your people with information, you empower them to have the responsibility to do the right thing. If you tell them how your company makes its money and where profits come from, they can better assess a customer's special request. They tend to see things more from the "big picture" when they know more. Give your people "...solid knowledge of the company..." so they are..."well informed, make sound decisions, and have a flexible, creative problem-solving approach." (NUTS!)

A little bit more knowledge goes a long way. Give people the information and tell them how it fits into the big picture. Tell them why they wouldn't announce a hotel guest's room number across the room.

3. Make it Easy for People to Learn by Example

Southwest matches new employees with senior people who are KNOWN for giving good service. "People at Southwest do the right thing because that's who they are." (NUTS!) Make living legends out of your service heroes. Real examples inspire others to offer legendary service, too. Think of your star service performers. What kind of matchmaking could you do to pair up your stars with up-and-coming stars? Let them watch and learn. Let them see how uncommon gestures of exceptional service can become common.

4. Let Common Sense Prevail

"We never jump on the employee for leaning too far in the direction of the customer." (NUTS!) Show people what legendary service looks like then trust them to do the right thing.

In a memo to Southwest's station managers: "No employee will ever be punished for using good judgment and good old common sense when trying to accommodate a Customer—no matter what our rules are. Let's start leaning toward out Customers again—not away from them."

Southwest managers reinforce the fact that we cannot always know what surprise circumstances will pop up, but that we can use our best judgment to handle them the best way we can. In return, they will let us know if we've gone a bit too far---without "...criticism, without backbiting." (NUTS!)

5. People Inspire People

"Publish stories of extraordinary service in your newsletter. If you don't have one, write them up in a letter to employees." (NUTS!)

Where do you post kudos about your people? If you don't have a newsletter, how about an online e-zine? Or how about a web page on your site designated for kudos only. You could even let your employees give their kudos to their fellow staffers via a bulletin board (online or wall-mounted). There's always a place to praise service over and above normal—and people need to hear about it so they can duplicate it or better it.

6. Help Ordinary People Do Extraordinary Things.

"Make it a practice to give everyone—customers, co-workers, friends, family—more than they expect." (NUTS!)

Practice the baker's dozen theory (one extra donut or bagel) than the customer expects---and it's FREE! Get your people to brainstorm extras that would fit in with your culture. Make a list and circulate it. Celebrate their ability to give when the time is right. Help them understand when that time is. Let them share their extra stories and watch their eyes light up.

Does Southwest's customer culture work? The numbers speak volumes to answer that question: They've gone from 4 planes in 1971 to 243 (1996), from 195 employees to 22,944, from 108,554 passengers to 49,621,504, from 3 cities served to 50, from a stockholder's equity of $3,318,000 to $1,648,312,000 (1996). (NUTS!)

I've long been a fan of T. Scott Gross's Positively Outrageous Service. In the book, he lists "Twenty-Five Service Attributes Ranked in Order of Importance to Customers," from Linda Cooper, head of First Chicago Bank's consumer affairs. Even though some of these are skewed toward banking customers, some still ring true of many customers:

1. Being called back when promised
2. Receiving explanation of how a problem happened.
3. Providing me with information so I know what number(s) to call.
4. Being contacted promptly when a problem is resolved.

5. Ability to talk to someone in authority.
6. Being told how long it will take to solve a problem.
7. Being given useful alternatives if a problem can't be solved.
8. Being treated as though I am a person, not an account number.
9. Being told about ways to prevent a problem in the future.
10. Being given progress reports if a problem can't be solved immediately.
11. Ability to talk to the service representative without interruption.
12. Not being put on hold without asking me.
13. Being treated with appreciation for my business.
14. Having an actual person answer my call rather than a recording.
15. Being told the service Representative's name and telephone number.
16. Getting through to the customer service department on the first call.
17. Being offered suggestions on how to keep my costs of banking services down.
18. Ability to speak with someone on the first call who has the authority to solve a problem.
19. Receiving an apology when an error is made.
20. Being helped without being put on hold.
21. Having a phone answered by the third ring.
22. Being greeted with "Hello" or "Good morning."
23. Ability to reach the service area after 4:00 p.m.
24. Being addressed by my name.

25. Ability to reach the service area before 8:30 a.m.

(Excerpted from T. Scott Gross's Positively Outrageous Service, Warner Books, 1991)

These serve as reminders of what our customers are telling us they want. Practice customized service by finding out exactly what is important to your customers...and DO IT!

CHAPTER ELEVEN

Follow Up And Flourish

How to Stack the Deck So Customers Choose You Over the Competition.

Rhonda Wildman

Rhonda Wildman began developing her "Take Charge!" technique in first grade. She became the "Top Cookie" in her girl Scout troop by selling the most cookies in her region.

Rhonda soon discovered that commissions were more lucrative than merit badges. For more than 20 years she has been a sales leader for such industry giants as Lanier and Johnson & Johnson.

Now she uses her expertise in superb service as a much sought after keynote speaker and seminar leader. She will inspire, instruct, and intensify your efforts for immediate results!

Simply put, "Take Charge!" is the formula that will reveal to your team the very best techniques to increase their productivity. YOU can make the difference by rising above and beyond expectations!

Take Charge!, LLC
Plano, TX • 888-265-9660 • www.takechargewithrhonda.com

Rhonda Wildman

Follow Up And Flourish

How to stack the deck so customers choose you over the competition.

Would you believe that between 65% and 85% of customers who choose a new supplier professed themselves satisfied or very satisfied with their old supplier? What does this mean to you? What can you do to make sure or to stack the deck so that your customer will continue to choose "YOU" over your competitors? The answer is two simple words FOLLOW UP. In today's highly competitive market, you must have something to differentiate yourself positively from the competition. A good way to do it is by providing superior and personalized service. In a world full of machines, everyone appreciates personal attention. Just read a few of the following ten documented reasons why following up is important.

WHY FOLLOWING UP IS IMPORTANT

1. A 5% increase in customer retention translates into a nearly 50% increase in growth and profits.

2. It can cost up to 5 times more to attract a new customer than to retain an existing one.

3. Suppose your company's advertisement budget is $100. It costs $20 to acquire a new customer while it costs $4 to retain an existing customer. How do you get the best return on your investment?
   Take Plan A into consideration: Acquire 4 new customers

and retain 5 existing ones. (4 x $20) + (5 x $4) = $100 for a net gain of 9 customers.
Now, take Plan B into consideration: Acquire 3 new customers and retain 10 existing ones. (3 x $20) + (10 x $4) = $100 for a net gain of 13 customers. Translation: higher unit profit margin and higher absolute profit level as well. The advantage of retaining existing customers is obvious.

4. On average, 96% of unsatisfied customers will not return.

5. For every complaint received, the average company has 26 customers with problems, 25% of those are serious.

6. Surprisingly, people who have problems and complain are more likely to do business with you again than non-complainers. This holds true even if the complainer's problem was unsatisfactorily resolved.

7. Of customers who register a complaint, between 54% to 70% percent will do business again only if their complaint is resolved. The number goes up to an astounding 95% if the customer believes that the complaint was resolved quickly.

8. The average customer who has a problem with an organization tells 9 to 10 people about it.

9. 13% of the people who have a problem with an organization recount the incident to an average of 22 people.

10. Customers who have complained to an organization and have had their complaints satisfactorily resolved inform an average of 5 people about their experience.

To help you rise above the statistics, here are ten great ways to follow up. These are proven methods that build relationships, increase credibility, build trust, differentiate you from the competition, and solidify your relationship with your customers. Everyone appreciates appreciation. You can make someone's heart smile by letting them know they are valued. A little personalized attention goes a long way. Not only does it let the customer know that you are interested in building a solid business relationship, but also that you are concerned with their satisfaction.

All things considered, remember that your customer's time is very valuable to them. Don't waste it! You should not be sending extensive proposals (unless requested), instead the follow up should be short and to the point.

TEN GREAT WAYS TO FOLLOW UP

1. Phone Call

This personal method is easy, requires little time and is inexpensive. Most effective results occur from appointed calls. Prior to calling, work with the customer to specify a date and time to follow up. The customer now puts you ahead of your competitors. Customers quickly open more opportunities to you knowing you take action and serious interest in them and their business.

2. E-mail

Very simple and quick, remember to keep it brief and personal. When you are dealing with electronics, you are taking the human interaction out of the relationship. Be sure to add the human touch. Keep it warm, yet professional. Here are a few fun things called smileys to put within your text. :) ;) :o ^^

3. E-greeting

Entertaining and personalized! You can customize your greeting to fit the individual's personality, line of work, and hobby. Several sites allow you to send musical greetings.

4. Postcards

Hand-written or pre-typed, make this a fun way to follow up and provide a piece they'll keep around or even show-off to co-workers. For example, print important sporting event schedules, inspirational quotes, useful information, or a humorous picture on the card. Purchase these from a store or make your own. Create them using fun photographs you've taken or software.

5. Thank You Note

Invest in personal stationery and envelopes. Always hand write these notes so that they look personalized. If your writing is ugly, illegible or both, have someone with good penmanship write the note for you. Brief, yet personal makes a lasting impression.

6. Personal Letter

This is a more formal way to follow up. Type the letter on a company or personal letterhead using proper format. For a more aesthetic appearance, try heavy stock (28 lb.) watermarked paper.

7. Flowers

Brighten their day with flowers. You can get everyone in the office talking. What a great way to send a ripple effect of good spirits. It enhances the atmosphere and gives the whole office one more reason to continue doing business with you. Send anything from a single flower to a full-size bouquet. To ensure the freshness of the flowers, use a guaranteed service.

8. Munchies

The way to customers' pocket books is through their cravings for carbohydrates. Send a candy-gram, cookie bouquet, or party platter to let them know you are serious about their business. Once you give food they always want more! This can start an addiction to doing business with you. To get more food, they will do more business.

9. Donations

For the bottom line person, who has everything and is being barraged by everyone, send a donation. Most non-profit organizations like the American Cancer Society have beautiful donation gift cards they will send out for you for any occasion. Contact them by phone or go to their Web site and give the person's name, address and reason for sending and they do the rest. In the medical industry, I knew I could not compete with all the lavish gifts the doctors' offices were receiving. So I made a contribution in honor of each doctors' office to the American Cancer Society. Not only, did it set me apart from my competition every holiday season, but also attracted new opportunities and further endeared me to existing customers. It impresses them more if you send a donation in their honor to their favorite charity. Send one to your favorite charity if you don't know, or they don't have one.

10. Logo Collectables

Calendars, planners, pens, laser pointers, stress balls, CD holders, key chains, Swiss Army knives, polo-style shirts, mouse pads, etc. The list is inexhaustible. When you match a gift to something your customer wants or likes, it makes a long-lasting impression. It also spreads the word to others as they admire or comment on the gift. Sending a logo collectible ensures that you are within sight and mind all year.

EFFECTIVE AND EFFICIENT FOLLOW UP

How can you be effective and efficient with your Follow Up? Immediately put a Follow Up System in place! To help you get started take a look at the following three Follow Up finds:

Personal Digital Assistants (PDA)

These palm-sized organizational wizards can do it all. The selection can be overwhelming. I still use an original Palm III. I love it and it does everything I need it to do. Sure companies have come out with smaller, powerful, Internet accessible, color screens, etc. Even with all the market advancements, my Palm III continues to keep me on the top of my game.

Pick and choose according to your budget, needs and wants. Consumer Reports is a great place to start your search for the best PDA for you. Also, check out PDA opinion Web sites like www.geek.com and www.the-gadgter.com. Convenience, without a doubt, is the PDA's salient benefit. Many PDAs are so small and lightweight they'll fit into your pocket and you can carry them anywhere. And they perform numerous organizational functions — fast. It's great having your critical contact information at your fingertips. My PDA turned my frantic mess of notes into an organized information machine.

Contact Management Program

Your PC probably already has several of which to choose. Such programs have templates for letters, memos, faxes, brochures, etc. You can also design your own. Most programs have publishing wizards making it easy for even the computer-shy person. Save letter templates on your computer so that all you have to do is enter their name and sign it.

Notebook Organizers

Effective and inexpensive, these notebooks allow you to keep up with your daily activities and business tasks. However, if you plan on expanding your business, you may want to invest in something more.

Pick the system that is most comfortable for you and that you will use! Don't get caught up in making it so unique or extravagant, that's not important. What is important is that you have a system in place.

Remember, the time you are investing in setting up a follow up system will pay off short-term and long-term. Customers will go out of their way to protect your business. In my case, having a follow up system in place paid off by giving me the largest single order in the history of the company. It started with my guarantee to customers that I would respond to a page in five minutes or less. The customers loved testing my guarantee and were impressed that I delivered. They paged me when a competitor tried to woo them and asked, "Will you give us service like this?" They barely hung up and I would have already returned their call. I was known as "Ready Rhonda" and had a perfect track record.

A nurse I worked with over the years took a new position as an Operating Room Supervisor at a brand new hospital. This hospital was only supposed to use national contract vendors. Unfortunately, I was not one of those vendors. Follow up was so important to her; it was worth the tedious process she had to follow to justify the use of an unlisted contractor. This is one of the many success stories of following up. My 21 years of award-winning sales is based on this one key factor: FOLLOW UP!

How Other Companies Follow Up

What have other people done to follow up? Of course, there are the likes of Marriott, who hired staff to assess customer satisfaction. They have increased their core business by 50% by doing this. I've experienced similar follow up situations first-hand.

Ray Huffines Chevrolet, in Plano Texas takes follow up seriously. Every time I have my car serviced there, the dealership customer service follows up within two days. They are ready and eager to document my satisfaction and ask for improvement suggestions. Since the car is registered in my husband's name, they always asked for him. I explained that I drove the car and to ask for me whenever they call. I appreciated their paying attention to the request and by personalizing their follow up system for me. Does that make me a more endeared customer to them? You bet. That was the second car I had purchased from that dealership.

Follow up is what brings people back, not the negotiation of the deal but the service after. Once the ink dries on the check, what determines repeat business is the subsequent treatment the customer receives.

Make it Happen

Do you want to quickly build credibility? Do you want to have repeat business and build long lasting business relationships with your customers? How about having the customer think of you first when starting a project? You can make it happen with one easy step: Follow Up!

You are now armed with ten great ways to get started with your system. As an anonymous quote states, "To know and not to do is to not know at all." Now you know and, now you must do. Follow Up and Flourish!

CHAPTER TWELVE

Create A Service Culture-- Talk Is Cheap!

An Eight-Step Action Plan to Build A Service Culture

Barbara Sanfilippo, CSP, CPAE

Barbara Sanfilippo, CSP, CPAE, helps companies unite all staff and departments to enhance service, accelerate sales and improve performance. Her enthusiastic and entertaining style combined with her "how to," idea-packed programs have earned her the respect and repeat business of CEOs, associations and corporations in a variety of industries both nationally and internationally. In addition to speaking, her consulting and training company, Romano & Sanfilippo, LLC, partners with organizations to build a sales and service culture by implementing a comprehensive action plan.

Barbara is the author of *Dream Big! What's The Best That Can Happen?* and is one of 73 speakers worldwide to receive both the prestigious Certified Speaking Professional (CSP) designation and the CPAE Speaker Hall of Fame award given by the National Speakers Association. Whether speaking to executive management, business owners, sales representatives or support staff, Barbara has the unique gift of tailoring a message that's right on target.

Barbara Sanfilippo, CSP, CPAE
Escondido, CA • 760-738-9100 • www.RomanoSanfilippo.com

Barbara Sanfilippo, CSP, CPAE

Create A Service Culture--Talk Is Cheap!

An Eight-Step Action Plan to Build a Service Culture

"We've been working on our service culture for many years now and we just haven't gotten the results we expected."

All too often we hear CEOs, senior managers and business owners voicing similar frustrations at their efforts to develop a service culture throughout their company.

What undermines many organizations' efforts at developing a service culture is thinking they can simply run their people through customer service or "smile" seminars and hand out customer comment cards.

In other words, many companies look for a "quick fix" which only yields short-term results. If you want a "customer-focused" process, it takes a well thought out plan and commitment from every person and department in your entire company. Following is an eight-step action plan you can use to build the "infrastructure" necessary to sustain your service culture.

1. SHARE THE VISION AND GET STAFF INVOLVEMENT

How high a priority is building a service culture in your company? Does your staff have a sense of urgency about delighting your customers and building relationships?

To become a reality, the development of a service culture must be an integral part of a CEO's vision. Following are some practical ideas to share the vision:

- Hold an off-site retreat with your management team and key managers to discuss your service philosophy and to strategize the action plan in this chapter.
- Make sure your strategic plan identifies "building a service culture" as an objective.
- Host a fun, all-staff "kickoff" event to communicate both your vision and your service action plan to all associates.
- Create a permanent "Service Council" that includes your management team and representation from each area of your company. Council members meet monthly and coordinate implementation of your action plan, serve as team leaders, identify obstacles and generally act as "champions."
- Utilize Service Improvement Teams™ (SITs™) to implement items in your action plan for the eight components listed here. Allow three to four months for each team to complete their project. Ask a member of your Service Council to head up each team to demonstrate their support and leadership.
- Next invite employees to serve on the varying teams to encourage buy-in and commitment.

In summary, to build a strong foundation for your service culture, make it a strategic objective, share your vision and get your people involved.

2. DEVELOP QUALITY SERVICE STANDARDS

Ever wonder why you prefer certain hotels, stores or restaurants? Good chance it's because they consistently meet or exceed your expectations. The key word is consistently. If we want to keep our customers for life, we also need to provide consistent service by developing service standards.

We recommend you develop both internal standards between departments and external standards to your customers. Ask your staff to interview their internal associates to determine their service expectations and then establish standards. A standard is specific, measurable and verifiable. For example, a "weak" internal standard for a data processing department is, "Support our frontline staff as best we can." A better standard is, "When the computer is down, notify all offices and departments of system status on an hourly basis." Internal standards ensure operational excellence.

Likewise, we need to ask our external customers what they expect and turn their expectations into quality service standards. For example, a "weak" external standard is, "All customer calls will be returned promptly." A better standard is, "All customer calls will be returned within two hours. If you do not have an answer in the promised time, call the customer and give them an update."

Form your first Service Standards SIT™ and get your staff participating in the process. Remember to have your Service Council review the draft standards before they are finalized.

3. OFFER SERVICE TRAINING AND REINFORCEMENT

Invest in training your staff to deliver excellent service, which will increase your bottom line and customer referrals. Service impacts sales and customer retention. In addition to a "customer service" formal class, try the following ideas.

Offer Product Knowledge Training

Customers will purchase more services when those services fill their needs. Employees who thoroughly understand how your products provide solutions will sell more and provide added value to your customers.

Reinforce Product Knowledge in Fun and Challenging Ways

- Consider a team game like "Jeopardy" in which questions have a specific point value. Create teams consisting of your best product knowledge experts and have an "Olympics of Product Knowledge" game.
- Offer a "Product-of-the-Month" quiz that rewards employees for proficiency in a particular product or service.
- Ask a SIT™ to create a product knowledge manual that outlines benefits, features, cues, open probing questions, objections and a contact person for each product/service. The key is to give your staff the key questions that will allow them to start a conversation comfortably with a customer.

- Offer brown bag "munch and learn" sessions once a month and, if you can, provide a light lunch.

Many of our clients have found that a solid "product knowledge program" positively impacts staff confidence, customer service and sales performance.

Host A Customer Panel

At staff meetings or quarterly sales meetings invite three or four customers to participate in a panel discussion. Ask such questions as:

- What does excellent customer service mean to you?
- What do we do well and how can we improve?
- What is our competitor doing to get your business?

After your CEO or moderator finishes the formal questions to the customers, allow 20-30 minutes for your staff to ask questions.

Schedule Service Field Trips

Ask your staff and managers to visit or call both excellent service companies and your competitors to rate the service and present their findings to the Service Council. This is an excellent way to reinforce your service philosophy and desired behaviors.

4. MEASURE INTERNAL AND EXTERNAL SERVICE

A survey conducted by the International Customer Service Association found that of customers who had a negative experience with a company and subsequently complained, 54% continued to do business with the company long-term. Of those who had a problem and did not complain, only 9% continued to do business with the company. Therefore, it is important to give your customers the opportunity to critique your service. Some suggestions for your Service Measurement SIT™ are:

- Measure the level of internal service provided between departments. Once internal service standards are developed (see 2 above), you can measure your internal service by distributing a quarterly Inter Departmental Service Inquiry™ (IDSI™) to your staff. This will increase communication as support and frontline areas work together to resolve issues.

- Hire a firm to conduct regular mystery shopping in person or by phone. Alternatively, ask your customers to critique a service interaction and fill out a survey asking: Did we acknowledge you? Serve you courteously? Use your name? Thank you?
- Designate quarterly "customer feedback weeks." Each quarter ask your staff to proactively hand out "Tell Us How We Are Doing" cards. Use a numerical system ranking each question on a 1-5 scale so you can develop a customer satisfaction index (or CSI) for your team or company.

Ask your SIT™ to submit their service measurement ideas to the Service Council.

5. RECOGNIZE AND REWARD YOUR SERVICE SUPERSTARS

Recognition is one component that many employees consistently rate poorly on our sales and service climate survey. When your employees feel unappreciated, their motivation to enthusiastically serve customers is reduced.

Once you are measuring service (see 4 above), it's easy to design a Service Recognition Club. For example: Any office or customer service representative receiving a service score of at least 85% on the random sampling survey gets into the Silver Club and a score of 95% gets into the Gold Club.

Reward support departments for providing excellent internal service to other departments and associates. This is measured by distributing the IDSI™ mentioned in #4 and rewarding those departments with a high score. For example, any department getting at least 25 points on the IDSI™ gets a team party. Also fun "Gotcha" or "Thank You" praising coupons are a great way for associates to reward one another "on-the-spot."

The Recognition SIT™ has one of the most enjoyable assignments and is encouraged to get input from other staff members.

6. HOLD PEOPLE ACCOUNTABLE FOR SERVICE!

By now, you've spent considerable time and money on creating standards, measuring service, providing training, developing product knowledge programs, and much more. Protect your investment by setting service goals and holding people accountable for results.

Tighten up your goal setting and performance appraisal review process. Assign a "weighting" and define the percentage of the job devoted to service and product knowledge.

For example: A manager can have the following objective and weights assigned in their performance appraisal for service:

Achieve a customer satisfaction score: 25%

- 90% or higher — Excellent
- 85-89% — Good
- 75-84% — Average
- 74% or less — Unsatisfactory

Achievement of at least 85% on product knowledge quizzes: 25%

Service goals are measured for a team and individuals based on either random sampling, comment cards, mystery shopping, on the spot customer surveys, etc.

For example: A support department manager can have the following service objectives:

Achieve an Inter Departmental Service Inquiry™ score in serving your fellow associates as follows: 30%

- 25 points or higher — Excellent
- 20-24 points — Good
- 15-19 points — Average
- 14 or less points — Unsatisfactory

Goals and accountability are essential to keep your service culture alive. We consider it a key success factor in working with our clients.

7. DEVELOP A CUSTOMER RETENTION AND APPRECIATION PROGRAM

Today's fiercely competitive environment demands that we "protect" our best customers. Some of your best customers are on your competitor's prospect list. By touching your customers when they least expect it, you can create a sense of loyalty.

For example, six months ago much to my surprise, a lady named Emma called from my local bank branch. She enthusiastically announced, "My name is Emma and I'm happy to inform you that you and Bob have been identified as 'premier banking' customers, and I am your personal banker."

Since that call, she has sent us a CD of classical music, given us tickets to a volleyball tournament and quickly approved us for a line of credit.

I must say, prior to Emma's call, we did not feel particularly loyal to this bank and were thinking of leaving. Create a Customer Retention and Appreciation SIT™ to protect your customers and ask them to:

- Identify those at risk customers you cannot afford to lose.
- Assign these VIP customers to your managers and staff. Ideally, your staff will each have their own book of business to develop and manage.
- Begin an outreach program by calling each VIP customer and introducing yourself. Find out their interests, birthday, potential needs and service satisfaction and enter it in your contact management system or customer profile.
- Develop "value-added" items such as discount coupons, educational seminars, express service and other customer appreciation gestures.

8. DEVELOP A SPECIAL ORIENTATION PROGRAM

Now that you have implemented many components of a service culture, it's time to take a look at your employee orientation program. We suggest you form an Orientation SIT™ and ask some key questions:

- What does our orientation process include? When hired, what will a new employee be told about our company, its culture, its values and its expectations?
- Does our orientation process include references to our mission statement, vision and service philosophy? Does the orientation include an explanation of our sales and service culture and performance expectations?

Some suggestions for your "Orientation Team" are as follows:

- Be sure to invite one or two recently hired employees to serve on your team since their orientation is fresh on their mind.
- Ask each team member to identify a local and national organization that has a reputation for service excellence, such as Marriott or Hyatt Hotels, and call them for a phone interview. Ask what they do to build their service philosophy into their orientation.
- Take a new employee to lunch within the first two weeks and designate a "buddy" in the department.
- Ask all new hires and existing support staff to spend a half-day visiting frontline staff members to observe what it's like to serve customers.
- Develop a handbook for each new employee with your organizational chart, mission statement and vision, values, service standards, key products, service measurement tools and other helpful exhibits.
- Set a follow-up date for your CEO or human resource coordinator to meet with each new hire within 30-60 days to get an honest assessment of how they are doing, if they are happy or if they need any additional support.

Whether you are a small or large company, it's important to share your expectations and vision with all new associates. By instilling pride in your new associates, you have a better chance of attracting and retaining the best people.

SUMMARY

I'm sure you can see the value of taking an "organizational approach" to building your service culture. Service is not a destination – it's a journey. In fact, you should allow one to two years to implement the above action plan. Our most successful clients have a permanent "Service and Sales Council" and still form Service Improvement Teams™ or SITs™ as necessary.

By implementing the eight-step action plan outlined here with staff involvement, you will create a strong service culture that ultimately impacts long-term revenue, improves teamwork and delights your customers.

THE
SERVICE
PATH
Additional Resources From
Our Team Of Co-Authors

Additional Resources from Tracy Brown

BOOKS

Breaking the Barrier of Bias	$14.95
Tracy's Top Tips: Transforming Awareness to Action (1/01)	$15.00

AUDIO CASSETTES

The R Word: Succeeding In Spite of Racism	$10.00
Breaking the Barrier of Bias (4 Tape Set)	$35.00
motiVersity: Motivating While Valuing Diversity (2 Tape Set)	$20.00
Maximizing Diversity in Health Care Settings (6 Tape Set)	$75.00

ORDERING INFORMATION:

Person To Person Consulting
Tracy Brown
Dallas, Texas
Toll Free: 1-888-316-4447
214-369-2888
www.TracyBrown.com

Additional Resources from Regina Clark

AUDIO CASSETTES

Spice Up Your Speaking: How to Keep an Audience Awake During a Technical Presentation (2 audio cassettes & tip sheet) $19.95

ORDERING INFORMATION

Clark Training & Development
PO Box 383
Goshen, NY 10924
845-294-7089
clarktrain@aol.com

Additional Resources from Tiger Harrison

VIDEO PROGRAMS
"Awaken the Tiger in Your Service Organization" (Tiger's most requested keynote presentation) How to get your service staff on the same page and develop standards they own.
"Avoiding Blackout Blues...Turning on Powerful Employees"
24-7-365...How do you boost morale and productivity in today's constant - no end in sight business environment? Learn tools to work more effectively with all four generations.

Video & Reference Guide - $129.00

AUDIO CASSETTES
"Awaken the Tiger in Your Service Organization"
"Taming the Tigers - Dealing with Difficult & Demanding People"
"Avoiding Blackout Blues...Turning on Powerful Employees"

Single Cassettes & Action Plan - $29.95
3 Pack - $68.85

SPECIAL REPORTS
"What They Really Want" - Based on research with 3700 participants from Russia, the Ukraine, China, Panama, Puerto Rico, Canada, and the U.S. Find out what our global customers really want and the 12 things that will drive them away.
Full Report $74.95

PACKAGES
"Service Survival Pack" - (Front line staff) - $68.85
- "Awaken the Tiger in Your Service Organization" - Audio
- "Taming the Tigers - Dealing with Difficult & Demanding People"- Audio
- "The Service Path" - Book

"Tiger's Tool Chest" - (Managers) - $298.95
- "Avoiding Blackout Blues...Turning On Powerful Employees" - Video & Guide
- "Taming the Tigers - Dealing with Difficult & Demanding People" - Video & Guide
- Special Report - "What They Really Want" - Full Report (1 yr of quarterly updates)

ORDER INFORMATION:
RS Harrison International /TigerTalk.com
San Ramon, California
925-798-4751
www.TigerTalk.com

Additional Resources from Jana High

AUDIO CASSETTES
Networking: Basic Tips for Effective Networking (1 audio cassette) $10.00

VIDEO TAPES
Customer Service: How to Develop the "WOW" by Delivering Exceptional Customer Service (2 video cassettes and workbook) $59.95

BOOK
High-Tech Etiquette: Perfecting the Art of Plugged-In Politeness (publication expected in Feb. 2002) $20.00

ORDERING INFORMATION
JLH Presentations
3020 Legacy Drive, Suite 100-310
Plano, TX 75023
866-820-6303 Toll-Free
972-516-1510 FAX
jana@jlhpresentations.com

Additional Resources from Michael Hoffman

AUDIO PROGRAMS

"It's All in a Day's Work"

Ignite your customer service people to Super Hero performance with this hilariously motivational session recorded live at the International Customer Service Association's Annual Representative Appreciation night.

CD: $15.00 Audio Cassettes: $10.00

AUDIO / VIDEO WORKSHOP

"Sales Secrets of the One Percenters" seminar workshop

Is a "how to" presented by four top sales professionals who are leading the pack in their industries. They'll share their secrets, tips and techniques that keep them in the top 1%. This four-volume set will teach you, step-by-step, how to unlock your own performance power, ignite your sales and equip you with the tools you need to achieve your highest aspirations for success.

Videos: $150.00 includes four videos plus manual

Cassettes: $65.00 includes four audio cassettes

ORDER INFORMATION:

M. Hoffman Enterprises, Inc.

2415 Via Del Sur

Carrollton, TX 75006

972-389-1800

www.ignitingperformance.com

Additional Resources from JP Maroney

AUDIO CASSETTES
Business Builders...Business Busters (JP's most requested keynote presentation) How to leverage your organization's human capital. (single cassette) $9.95

Achieving Excellence Personally & Professionally: The qualities, characteristics and motives of exceptional human beings. (single cassette) $9.95

VIDEO PROGRAMS
Business Builders...Business Busters (JP's most requested keynote presentation) How to leverage your organization's human capital. (single video) $59.95

Achieving Excellence Personally & Professionally: The qualities, characteristics and habits of exceptional human beings. (single video) $59.95

EMPLOYEE CONTINUOUS PERFORMANCE IMPROVEMENT SYSTEM
People Builders: Interactive, Monthly Audio/Video Learning Series
Receive a new learning module each month featuring a major topic for improving employee performance and productivity (eg: Customer Service, Team Building, Communication Skills). Train all of your employees (10, 100, or 1000) for one year subscription at only $149 per month + $5.50 S&H. Each monthly module includes: video, audio, participant handouts, posters, module feedback form, facilitator success guide, materials storage binder, free training tips, and more. Call for full details, or visit www.PeopleBuilders.com

POSTERS THAT REINFORCE LEARNING
(Packets of 5 powerful posters JP uses during his presentations)
Is 99.9% Good Enough? (11″x17″) $9.95
Business Builders...Business Busters (11″x17″) $9.95
Why Customers Don't Return (11″x17″) $9.95
12 Customer Service Strategies for the New Millennium (11″x17″) $9.95

ORDERING INFORMATION:
JP Maroney International
Tyler, Texas
1-800-304-5758
www.JPMaroney.com

Additional Resources from Bernadette Vadurro

VIDEOS

Effective Presentation Skills for Women (53 Minute)	$59.95
Customer Service Excellence (Video + Work book)	$795.00

AUDIO

Customer Service Excellence	$79.95

BOOK

Motivational Leaders "Strategies and Wisdom from America's Top Professional Motivators"	$14.95

SPECIAL PACKAGES

Compliance For I.H.S. and Tribal Health Care Facilities	$995.00

ORDERING INFORMATION:

Bernadette B. Trujillo-Vadurro
Leading Edge Training Technologies
821 Paseo de Don Carlos
Santa Fe, NM 87501
505-983-8986
1-800-736-8986 Toll Free
505-986-0055 FAX
www.letraining.com

Additional Resources from Kelli Vrla

AUDIO CASSETTES
SOME OF KELLI V'S MOST REQUESTED KEYNOTES:

"Bullet-Proof Your Life and Your Work: How to De-Stress for Success!"
This entertaining, enlightening, keynote provides more than 50 ways to humorize everyday stressors and "see" funny. It also offers a humor break and stress relief for all levels.
Available on Audio Cassette...........$ 15.00
Includes 1 FREE RED NOSE!

"Change: How to Be an Adept Adaptor"
Adaptability is the key to survival in a fast-paced world. This presentation shows steps to identify positive versus negative change and provides valuable, proactive techniques to turn adversity into competitive advantage.
Available on Audio Cassette.............$15.00
Includes 1 FREE RED NOSE!

"Humorific Customer Service: How to WOW Now!"
Differentiating yourself from the competition is simple: Focus on the "little" things that make doing business a fun experience for your customers. If you take care of the details, the dollars will take care of themselves. This innovative session promotes creative thinking, problem©solving and an enjoyable work environment.
Available on Audio Cassette.............$15.00
Includes 1 FREE RED NOSE!

RED NOSES & T-SHIRTS
RED NOSES.............. By the dozen...........Only $15.00
(Comfort foam: 2" diameter, ready-to-wear)

T-Shirt: "I Laughed with Kelli V and All I Got Was This Lousy T-Shirt"
$15.00
Includes 1 FREE RED NOSE!

Please add $3.00 Shipping and Handling

ORDERING INFORMATION:
Kelli S. Vrla
5521 Greenville Avenue, Suite 104-422
Dallas, Texas 75206
214.987.HA©HA (4242)
KSVrla@aol.com
www.kelliv.com

Additional Resources from Rhonda Wildman

TAKE CHARGE! TOOLS
POSTERS: ALL POSTERS COME IN PACKS OF 5

Attitude Poster (11x8.5)	$10.00
Vision Poster (11x8.5)	$10.00
Golden Goose Poster (11x8.5)	$10.00
Success is Never Accidental (11x8.5)	$10.00
Gold Standard (11x8.5)	$10.00
Generate Success worksheet (11x8.5)	$10.00

OTHER:

Take Charge! Live CD	$12.00
Take Charge! Live Audio Cassette	$10.00

SHIPPING & HANDLING:

$0-$25.00	$3.00
$25.01-$100.00	$8.00
$100.00-$200.00	$30.00
$200.01-$300.00	$40.00

Call for rates on purchases over $300.00.

ORDERING INFORMATION:

Take Charge!, L.L.C.
Rhonda Wildman
1-888-265-9660
214-663-8078
Plano, Texas

Additional Resources from Barbara Sanfilippo

CD/AUDIO CASSETTES OF BARBARA'S LIVE TELESEMINARS $18.00

- Develop Service Standards and Measure Service
- Develop A Customer Retention and Appreciation Program
- Pre Call Planning—Winning Sales Strategies of Top Performers!
- How to Build A Winning Sales Team—Sales Management Best Practices
- Master the Sales Call Process—A Self Evaluation
- Kick Your Sales Calling Team Into High Gear!
- Reward and Recognition Programs—Do's and Don'ts

BOOKS

- Dream Big! What's The Best That Can Happen? $13.00
- The Service Path: Your Roadmap For Building Strong Customer Loyalty $14.95

GUIDEBOOKLETS™ FOR SERVICE IMPROVEMENT TEAMS™ (see website)
INCLUDES INSTRUCTIONS AND SAMPLES FOR YOUR TEAMS

- Service Measurement (Internal and External)
- Service Standards (Internal and External)
- Performance Management (Goals/Accountability)
- Informal Recognition
- Formal Recognition
- Customer Retention and Appreciation
- Product Knowledge Certification

COMPREHENSIVE CONSULTING AND TRAINING (see website)

- Service and sales process includes GuideBooklets™, review of your work, attendance at our quarterly client Learning Community meetings, training classes, on site process reviews and more.
- Private Coaching By Phone (Sales and Service)
- Teleseminars (Email or call for schedule. $29-$49/person)
- Speaking, Training and Workshops
- Sales, customer service, life skills and motivational topics
- Facilitated Sales and Service Planning Retreats

ORDERING INFORMATION:

Barbara Sanfilippo
Romano & Sanfilippo
San Diego, CA
Toll Free:1-877-ISUCCEED
(760)738-9100
www.RomanoSanfilippo.com

Additional Copies of The Service Path

IF YOU WISH TO ORDER ADDITIONAL COPIES OF THE SERVICE PATH, CONTACT:

MaroCom Publishing Company
RE: The Path Series
PO Box 9492
Tyler, Texas 75711-9492
1-800-304-5758
www.PathSeries.com.com

*Volume discounts available

You can also find information on other titles in The Path Series at www.PathSeries.com